AF365040

First edition, 2024

Cover design by Jennie Lindell

ISBN (paperback)   978-91-989188-0-9
ISBN (e-book)   978-91-989188-1-6

Published by Andreas Lehner

Mind your money

A practical guide
to sustainable investments

Contents

Foreword

Money rules the world. This is an old saying, but it is becoming increasingly true in our current economic system of financial capitalism. I usually try to explain this to my students in two steps. First, consider the complexity of our modern economy. It no longer revolves around simple agricultural services which almost anyone can do, or handicraft products that people can make with their own hands. Such products and services typically do not require large investments in, for example, human capital (such as education) or physical capital (such as materials and machinery). Instead, our modern economy revolves around complex industrial and technological goods that require a combination of specialized workers and automated machines. Such products and services require much larger investments in terms of both human and physical capital, which in turn must be financed or paid for by financial capital.

Second, where is all that capital found nowadays? In an economic system that is dominated by private property rights, most of the capital would of course be held by individuals or corporations. However, the central meeting place of our system is what we call the capital market, which is the place where individuals and corporations that need capital can go to interact with other individuals or corporations that have some to spare. The capital market is the engine of our society since, as noted above, it is almost impossible to start or run a business without access to capital. So, it is basically on the capital market that all large decisions about our economy are being made. Therefore, money indeed rules the world.

Sustainable investment can be seen as a way of trying to harness the engine of the capital market for the sake of a better tomorrow. Because as long as money keeps flowing to industries and technologies that are harmful to people and the planet, it is difficult to see how society can change towards being more inclusive and sustainable. To address the current global challenges of climate change and absolute poverty, it is vital that money and capital flows towards business ventures that can play a more positive role in this development. According to a recent estimate, the energy sector alone may need investments of around 2.4 trillion USD per year, representing about 2.5% of the world GDP, to meet the Paris Agreement's target of a 1.5°C rise in global temperatures.

I have done academic research on the topic of sustainable investment for more than 15 years now. Being a philosopher and an economist, I have perhaps mostly been intrigued by theoretical questions such as how to understand the role of the capital market in contemporary society, and to what extent our ideas about suitable ethical principles and political regulations in the realm of finance may need to change. However, over the years I have also come to grapple with some more practical questions. Because an increasing number of individuals and corporations have started to ask me for concrete advice on where to invest their money, and I have also had to think about that question in relation to my own savings. Unfortunately, I have found that my theoretical insights only take me halfway in this respect. To really know about the most suitable alternatives that are available, one also needs more practical experience from the world of finance – a world that is constantly developing new concepts and products.

I am happy to say that the present book is very helpful with regards to the practical aspects of sustainable investment. Building on his own experience in the field – both from starting his own sustainable finance venture, and from investing in many others – the author can give very concrete advice to anyone that is interested in following his path. The book should be useful for both experienced and inexperienced investors, as well as for both those with lots of money to spare and those with more limited savings. It is acknowledged that redirecting your money towards more inclusive and sustainable businesses may not always have a large effect on the world, especially if you have a limited amount and there are other forces at play in the market. Moreover, we are all different and therefore different investment options may be suitable for your situation. But there is something to learn here for anyone that is interested.

Money rules the world, but it is ultimately investors – including individuals like you and me – who rule the money. We therefore have a responsibility to seek to put our money where it can do the most good for a better tomorrow. I recommend that you read this book and then try to do your part.

Joakim Sandberg

Professor of Practical Philosophy and Director of the Financial Ethics Research Group at University of Gothenburg / Economics and Finance from a Humanist Perspective at University of Groningen

Introduction

First, thank you for being interested in this book and the idea behind it. It is because of people like you that I still have hope for the future of our species. That might sound a bit dramatic, but we have big challenges ahead and need to make real change.

I started this journey years ago after watching Al Gore's first documentary "An Inconvenient Truth". It became clear that this is a challenge worth pursuing and dedicating my professional life to. Since then, many things have happened. I worked in electric mobility and solar energy, traveled to Kenya to get to know the sustainability issues there and co-founded my first company, Trine.

Trine builds a platform for sustainable investments, notable solar energy in emerging markets. Through working on Trine, I got to know that there is one major shift we need to make: Moving our money to more sustainable options.

I personally tend to have a black-or-white personality. I am either all-in or all-out. Therefore, as adapting the mindset of sustainability is crucial in this day and age, I changed my lifestyle completely. Becoming vegan/flexitarian, biking and not owning a car and traveling more environmentally friendly. I looked at investing with the same perspective and wanted to find sustainable investment options for myself. And I struggled to find suitable options and guidelines on how to do it.

After years of experimenting and adapting my approach, it is time to share what I have learned so far with a wider audience, with the hope that it will inspire more people to do the same.

Let's be clear from the beginning: Investing your money in sustainably is not the silver bullet to the myriad challenges we face as a human race. The obstacles before us are plentiful and complex and they require an unprecedented collaboration among all of us and cannot be solved by any one individual or act.

It is a powerful tool but just one of many ways we must make an impact. As we all know by now, our lifestyle choices are also important. But those choices can guide our investments and vice versa and have a broader impact.

While it can be easy to be discouraged, this book will provide you with a practical guide to support your investment and financial decisions. For that reason, I will not go into too much detail behind the research of sustainability, what climate change is, or how investing works. Because you are reading this book, I will assume that you know some of this information and are here looking for help on making sustainable investment decisions. What I will share with you is what has worked for me so far and what I have learned with a deeper understanding of how my financial assets can have a positive impact in the world. I am a practical person and have been looking for a guide on how to do my investments but couldn't find one. I hope this book eases that journey for you.

With climate change influencing literally every business sector and aspect of our lives, it is hard to find a reason *not* to invest sustainably. In fact, it is as imperative as any lifestyle choice you make right now.

It may seem impossible to truly know what to invest in because it seems daunting to assess the impact of your investments. While this book cannot solve every problem for you, I will attempt to provide a holistic idea of what sustainable investing is and how you could start doing it more concretely. I will also list assets that might not have a direct positive impact and whose positive impact can be argued about in long debates. I am doing this to offer you a holistic investment framework that includes different asset classes to diversify your risk. Sustainable investing also includes economic variables as it is called investing and not donating. These more sensitive assets will be marked clearly so you can make your own decision on if they are worth your consideration.

On that note, this book is not written in a way to give investment advice, but to empower you with more knowledge on how to make the best decision or to ask the right questions to a professional financial advisor. Please note that it is clear which of the suggested approaches in this book are more sustainable than others, but not 100 percent clear how sustainable each option is in and by themselves. You will be the final judge which assets you want to invest in and how strict and sustainable you want your portfolio to be.

Most of the services I am mentioning are products I have invested in myself and, as of this writing, had a positive experience. That does not guarantee that they will perform in the future. I just want to make a note that you are not obliged to use these services and products. None of them pays me to mention their name and I am not advertising for them. I have just used them for a while and am truly excited to share them with you.

The book is split into 5 parts, covering different topics.

Part 1 covers the question of **why** we want to invest sustainably. It will talk more generally about why sustainable investing is one of the best decisions you can make when it comes to climate change and why it is one of the best types of investment out there.

Part 2 will look more into **what** sustainable investing is, covering the three pillars of environmental, social, and economic sustainability.

In Part 3 we get more practical and look at the **how**. You will learn about how to get started, how to select a good investment and how to manage it.

Part 4 is going deeper into the **different assets,** and we finally get into the weeds. You will learn about different asset classes, from equity, commodities, real estate, art up to bonds. Here we will go quite detailed, explaining the impact of each asset and the different sub-segments and where you can find these asset classes. Please note that the practical parts here are quite Europe-focused and might not apply to your local context.

Part 5 is the wrapper for the previous parts and highlights different portfolios you could build, based on the asset classes you learned about in Part 4 and the extent of sustainability you want in your portfolio.

With that and a final conclusion, I hope that you have more tools in your arsenal to get out there and make your money work for the good of the world. I am grateful that you have chosen this book and hope it empowers you on your journey.

Lastly, I want to thank all the amazing people I have met along the way so far. You have inspired me to do things I would have never imagined and have shown me a way of aiming to become a better person over time. This book would not exist without the help of many of you, thank you!

Alright, it's time to get to it. Let's go!

I – Why Sustainable Investing?

We live in times of change. The current decade (2020-2030) will be a defining decade for humanity, whether we want it or not. We have the power to decide which change it will be, positive or negative. These coming years will determine our fate as a species and the fate of many other species on this planet that we call home. Why is that? Let's say we have not taken care of our house very well in the last century.

The Biggest Impact

To start off with, you might wonder "Why bother with sustainable investing? Shouldn't changing my lifestyle and living as environmentally conscious as possible be enough?" Well, we humans have one thing in common: we overestimate the impact of actions that are taken in our everyday life. Those might be simple such as separating our waste, eating less meat, or traveling less.

Comparing the impact of your actions taken in "real life" versus the impact of your investments shows a stark picture.

Nordea, a Swedish bank, did an analysis showing how investing more sustainably compares to some other more typical actions one can take.[1] They looked at four ways of reducing your impact that can have quite big impacts on your daily life:

- Shortening your showers from 5 minutes to two minutes
- Reducing our average long-distance flights from 2.7 times to 1.7 times a year
- Reducing the emissions from car travel by taking the train instead
- Eating only one piece of meat each week

If this is done over the working lifetime of an average Swede (42 years), you could save 1 ton of CO_2 for reducing your showering time, 19 tons of CO_2 by flying only 1.7 times per year, 26 tons of CO_2 by taking the train and 36 tons of CO_2 by eating less meat.

All together these four options you could save a whooping 82 tons of CO_2 - in TOTAL - over **42 years**. However, if you would put your finances into sustainable assets, you could save more than 2,200 tons of CO_2 in addition. That is 27 times more than the other four options combined! This assumes the average Swedish pension investment, which is roughly 1,100 EUR per year. If you invest more, the impact could be even higher! And it is relatively simple to maintain that positive impact once you have done the shift.

Divesting money might not be the one and only solution as removing your money from stocks that are not environmentally friendly means mainly that someone else will buy them. It depends a lot more on where you decide to invest your money after divesting, as additionality is only created once you support a company or initiative that would not have existed otherwise.

This shows clearly that if you want to change your impact on the environment you will have to investigate how you are investing. Don't get me wrong, both your direct emissions (the ones coming from driving a car or flying) as well as your indirect emissions (the ones coming from producing your meat and from your savings) matter. But the emissions from your investments are often overlooked and as all of us have only a limited time and brainpower to spend on these actions it makes sense to pick the most effective ones first.

Money Is Like Energy

I often tend to think of money as a concept of energy in our society. If you want to see where our society is focusing its attention, you just need to look at where it invests and spends its money and time. Like with energy or attention, where money flows, action and change happen.

Today, our societies are spending far too much on infrastructure that is not future-proof and non-sustainable such as gas pipelines or oil rigs. These investments are not only creating additional disasters such as oil spills, but also emissions that are pushing us even further into a climate crisis. Instead of increasing our greenhouse gas emissions, we need to start curbing them and walking (or better rushing) in the opposite direction.

And we - everyone - can affect this from the bottom-up. If we collectively acknowledge that unsustainable endeavors are not future-proof and that we would rather put our money into sustainable activities, we will set in motion a momentum that will be hard to stop. This is one of the many reasons that the divestment movement exists and has been successful. Big pension funds are already realizing this fact and are moving their capital to more sustainable and resilient assets as they need to think long-term for our generation's and our children's pension.

And as pension funds are clearly keeping in mind their return targets, there is also a financial side to investing sustainably.

It Is More Profitable

You might wonder: "Great, seems like sustainable investing for sure has a big impact. But I am investing and want to use my investments when I get older with a profit. I don't think this is for me?" Interestingly, however, companies that are leading in sustainability have shown themselves to be outperforming others with a poor ESG performance.

ESG means that one focuses one's assessment of a company on activities that have a positive effect on the **E**nvironment, **S**ociety and **G**overnance (basically how a company is run). Companies that have high ESG ratings generally are more sustainable and have fairer working conditions compared to the "normal" company in their sector.

According to a recent study the results of investments based on ESG criteria versus the traditional investment approach vary and are not homogenous across the board. But on average they are leaning towards the positive.

In some studies, these differences in performance are quite substantial. The ESG "stars" outperform the average sector company by over 4% p.a. According to RBC Global Asset Management, "the SRI (socially responsible investing) index SRI index has slightly outperformed the traditional index, although the differences are small. However, there can be meaningful differences, both positive and negative, over shorter periods (e.g., differences of +/- 2% over a one-year period are not uncommon, and they have been as large as 5%)."[2]

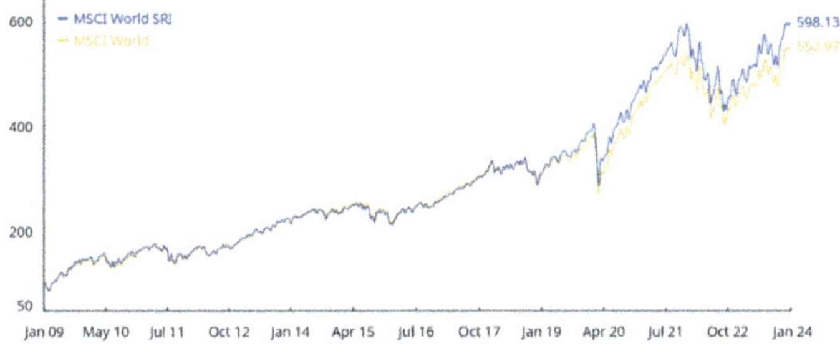

Figure 1 - US SRI Index Comparison with S&P500

Overall, it can be said that you will likely not lose return on your investments and probably gain slightly more. This also shows that the old mantra of "Doing good is charity" no longer holds. We live in a time where you can make money whilst doing good! This might seem too good to be true, but when you think about it, it makes sense. Companies that work with a sustainability mindset think more long-term, while many other companies tend to think very short-term which is one of the reasons we ended up in the current mess.

If you are investing in the long term (e.g. in your pension) it makes sense to bet on companies that do the same.

It Is the Future

If the paragraphs above haven't convinced you, one last thing is that there is hardly a way that sustainable investing is not going to become the new normal. Not only is it more profitable (on average) already today, but it is also the only way your investments can be future proof and be around for our pension in 20+ years.

Take for example a study done by the Financial Times.[3] In it they mentioned that in our current financial system if we were to keep a 1.5°C warming scenario, over 900 billion USD are invested in stranded assets such as oil, coal, and gas. This is around a third of all the fossil fuel assets out there. And 1.5°C will already have devastating effects. But even a 2°C warming target would leave 50% of fossil fuel assets worthless. These assets cannot be fully extracted if we want to avoid the worst impacts of climate change.

Therefore, companies that have these assets on their balance sheet cannot fully recover all the value that is priced in their stock prices. This will lead to a heavy stock price reduction and therefore the loss of a lot of investor value. Or we will have to deal with the worst effects of climate change which will have a way bigger impact on our society. Therefore, it makes logical sense to divest into more long-term viable assets.

McKinsey also wrote a report on the impact of climate change on the housing market in Florida.[4] In it the authors state the just a 1.5°C increase in global temperatures will lead to immense negative effects on the housing market in the US alone. Billions of dollars could be lost due to vast areas of land and real estate becoming unusable with rising sea levels.

And these effects could likely be extrapolated to other sectors such as the value of big supermarket chains when our food production cannot keep up with the demand or the value of car manufacturers that do not make the shift to more sustainable products or business models. Due to our economies being so complex and interconnected, we probably do not even foresee what the real effects will be when it comes to investment values being diminished.

Clearly investing in sectors that are being threatened by climate change to lose massively in value are not good long-term investments. Sustainable investing is your way out of this cycle, making your investments less dependent on these highly volatile assets and companies.

The Current Situation

So, what is the current situation when it comes to climate change, resource depletion and pollution?

Climate Change

Since we discovered fossil fuels and their power to use concentrated solar energy of the past (plants and dinosaurs that died millions of years ago) we have been on a tremendous growth trajectory.

In the span of 100 years, we quadrupled our population on this planet from around 1.5 billion people in 1900 to a bit over 6 billion people in 2000. At the same time, we doubled our life expectancy globally, from 35 years to 70 years on average.

Without access to fossil fuels this would not have been possible. However, now we are at a crossroads where we must look at the consequences of those actions. And one of the major issues, of many, is the effect that burning fossil fuels has on the climate.

When fossil fuels such as coal, oil or natural gas combust, they emit greenhouse gases. Most notably carbon dioxide and methane. The molecules of these greenhouse gases are relatively stable, and not only do they accumulate in our atmosphere, but they can stay there for decades or even centuries.

That by itself would not be an issue. However, these greenhouse gases are named like that for a reason. They trap heat in the atmosphere that otherwise would have been emitted back to the universe from Earth via infrared radiation. According to reports published by the Intergovernmental Panel on Climate Change (IPCC), human emissions of carbon dioxide and other greenhouse gases – are a primary driver of climate change – and present one of the world's most pressing challenges.[5] The IPCC was established in 1988 and is an intergovernmental body of the United Nation. It provides the world with objective, scientific information relevant to understanding the risk of human-induced climate change, its natural, political, and economic impacts and risks, and possible response options.

Over the last few decades, global temperatures have risen sharply — to approximately 0.7°C higher than our 1961-1990 baseline. When extended back to 1850, we see that temperatures then were a further 0.4°C colder than they were in our baseline. Overall, this would amount to an average temperature rise of 1.1°C.

In the following chart Figure 2 we see global average concentrations of CO_2 in the atmosphere over the past 800,000 years. Over this period, we see consistent fluctuations in CO_2 concentrations; these periods of rising and falling CO_2 coincide with the onset of ice ages (low CO_2) and interglacial (high CO_2).[6] These periodic fluctuations are caused by changes in the Earth's orbit around the sun – called Milankovitch cycles.

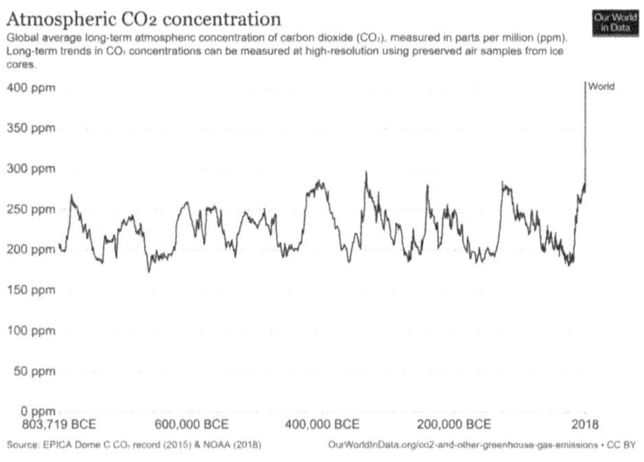

Figure 2 - Atmospheric CO₂ concentration

Over this long period, atmospheric concentrations of CO_2 did not exceed 300 parts per million (ppm). This changed with the Industrial Revolution and the rise of human emissions of CO_2 from burning fossil fuels. We have seen a rapid rise in global CO_2 concentrations over the past few centuries, and in recent decades. For the first time in over 800,000 years, concentrations did not only rise above 300ppm but are now well over 400ppm.

          The Current Situation

Not only have we managed to increase carbon emissions above historic levels, but we are also doing it at an unprecedented rate. Historical changes in CO_2 concentrations tended to occur over centuries or even thousands of years. We achieved even larger changes in a matter of decades only. This gives us and other species, planetary systems, and ecosystems much less time to adapt.

On the current trajectory set out in countries' own contributions, global temperatures will rise to at least 3°C by the end of the century.[7] As each degree of further warming will be proportionally more destructive, the damage will accelerate and be exponential. To avoid the most severe economic, social, and environmental consequences, climate experts warn that the temperature rise must be limited to 1.5°C.[8]

Why is the decade of 2020 so important?

In 2018, the IPCC estimated the remaining carbon budget for a 66% chance of avoiding 1.5°C of temperature rise was 420 gigatons of CO_2 – the equivalent of 10 years of global CO_2 emissions from fossil fuels and land-use change. We've got work to do.

Resource Depletion

We as a species do not live within the planetary boundaries of our planet. This means we consume more resources every year than can be regenerated by the environment.

We currently consume an equivalent of 1.6 planet resources every year. The initiative "Earth Overshoot Day" has defined that on the 2nd of August 2023 we had used the sustainable number of resources we can use in that particular year. Earth Overshoot Day marks the date when humanity's demand for ecological resources and services each year exceeds what Earth can regenerate in that year. We maintain this deficit by liquidating stocks of ecological resources and accumulating waste, primarily carbon dioxide in the atmosphere.

In 1970 we barely consumed more than the resources available to us, but over the years we have drastically changed this picture.

Pollution

In 2014, Americans produced about 258 million tons of solid waste, according to the U.S. Environmental Protection Agency.[9] A little over half of the waste — 136 million tons— was gathered in landfills. Only about 34% was recycled or composted.

Take plastic waste as an example. We increased plastic production 200-fold, from 2.3 million tons in 1950 to 448 million tons by 2015. About eight million tons of plastic waste escapes into the oceans every year. That's the equivalent of setting five garbage bags full of trash on every foot of coastline around the world.[10]

This plastic ends up in our oceans, endangering animals and entering food chains. It then gets broken down into microplastics, which are plastic pieces smaller than 5mm in size. These microplastics have been found all over the planet, from the Arctic snow and Alpine soils to the deepest oceans. Ultimately, they come back to us and enter our body by consuming them via food and water as well as breathing them in. We do not know the health effects yet, but they are most likely not positive, to say the least.

Many other industries are also polluting the environment, from major industries and manufacturers to mining companies. They can affect the quality of the air and the water in their close vicinity. In 2019, air pollution alone caused the premature death of nearly half a million babies in their first month of life, with most of the deaths being in emerging markets.[11]

They are also an integral part of the planetary boundaries and linked to both resource depletion, pollution, and climate change. The issues above are just the tip of the iceberg and by far not comprehensive nor exhaustive. For the sake of keeping this book solutions oriented I did not want to go too deep into each or even try listing a comprehensive summary of the problems we face. What I want to contribute is actual solutions to the issue, through the means of investing.

II - What is Sustainable Investing?

Sustainability has many faces and can often confuse people. In its essence it describes an activity which can be repeated without diminishing the conditions that are needed for that same activity to continue. Extracting resources at a speed that is in line with their natural replenishing is one way of defining an activity sustainable.

Definition

There are 3 pillars of sustainability when looking at investing as an activity. Environmental, social, and economic. Without these three pillars having sustainable elements one cannot talk about sustainable investing.

Sustainable investing is an investment strategy that combines financial gains with a focus on positive social and environmental impact. While "normal investing" only looks at the financial situation of a company or asset and has no other limiting factors, sustainable investing takes these factors into account when making an investment decision.

It is known by other names such as:

- Socially responsible investing
- Green investing
- Ethical investing
- Social investing
- Responsible investing
- Impact investing

These different terms refer to slightly different interpretations of a simple mantra:
Make money whilst doing good (socially or environmentally sustainable).

The spectrum of sustainable investing is quite wide, but there have been attempts to break down the range of investing approaches. One of the those comes from Sonen Capital and is pictured below.

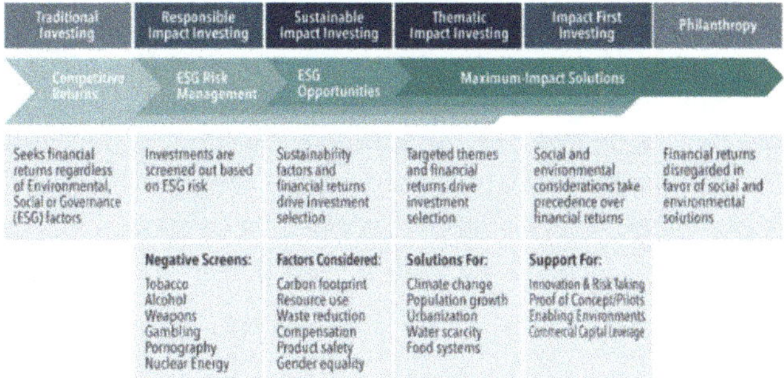

At one end of the spectrum, we have traditional, "business-as-usual' investing, which seeks financial returns with no impact focus at all. At the other end we have philanthropy, and an impact focus with no financial return expectation. In between is where the future lies and where impact is being created.

The first two categories after traditional investing are still focusing strongly on financial performance. But positive impact is beginning to become more important and a part of the investment assessment. Negative screening is used (more on that later), an approach which attempts to keep capital from being allocated to assets involved in "harmful" sectors of business. How that is defined is up to the investor or the fund, but some examples are given in the image above.

Sustainable Impact Investing
In Sustainable Impact Investing, ESG factors are considered alongside the financial return expectation. Capital is invested in assets which contribute positively to one or more of those ESG elements while also performing well financially. The idea is that investment opportunities that have good ESG scores will improve overall financial performance, and those with poor ESG scores will have poorer financial returns.

Thematic Investing
Thematic impact investing directs capital towards a defined focus area of impact with financial returns sought as a parallel priority. It is common for investors to focus their impact on areas that they are

passionate about, thus making them construct their portfolio around this impact-seeking ambition.

For example, an investor may identify lack of access to clean energy as one of the biggest issues of humanity and therefore focus their investments primarily on solutions addressing this need. Another way of breaking down themes could also be to look at regions, for example, focusing investments on Sub-Saharan Africa.

Impact-first Investing

This investment area focuses on positive impact as the driver of investment decisions. Financial returns remain to be a factor, but not a dominating one. This impact first approach often requires a higher risk tolerance on the financial side, such as targeting early-stage start-ups or solutions which have not been fully validated but which have a tremendous impact potential.

The investment could also take shape of patient capital into an asset, where the priority is the social or environmental impact and financial returns are either going to be below market rate and/or paid back over relatively lengthy periods of time. An example here would be many of the reforestation investment opportunities.

Environmental Sustainability

We've already determined that you want to ensure that you invest in assets that are having either a zero impact on the environment or making it better.

Environmental impact includes greenhouse gas emissions, environmental pollution, and resource depletion, among other factors.

As mentioned previously, to comply with this area you could invest in some of the following:

- Renewable energy projects or companies such as solar or wind
- Companies that make products that are better alternatives to what is on the market, such as circular business models, products that use less plastics or are more often reusable
- Reforestation projects that aim to restore forests in a sustainable fashion

To get more clarity around this segment when you are making an investment decision, you can ask yourself any of the following questions.

Emissions

Will your investment reduce emissions of greenhouse gases?
How will it reduce greenhouse gases?

This can be rather complex as you likely do not have the time to go into detail. Transparent companies often offer this information easily available, which you can consider in your analysis. You might want to consider the company's/project's material (what is it made of), production processes (how is it produced), logistic chains (how is it transported to consumers) and lifetime/warranty (is it a consumable product or is it made to last a long time)?

The more of these questions you can answer positively, the better its environmental impact likely is.

Pollution

Will your investment reduce pollution of any kind, for example plastic?

Like emissions, you want to understand what materials are being extracted, used and how recyclable these are. For example, investing in a product that is made from ocean plastic helps reduce the waste streams and reuse what is already there. Or products made of bioplastic do not need plastic in the first place and often decompose over time, leaving behind minimal trace (in the best scenario).

Resource Depletion

Will your investment reduce the resource intensity of products?
Will it support promoting alternative products or business models that can provide the same service while requiring less input?

Not only what we put out into the ecosystem has an impact. Equally important is how fast we use existing resources and how that rate of consumption compares to their rate of renewal. Here again, investing in companies producing goods out of waste or other recycled material is an option to invest in. Or companies with business models that have an in-built incentive to reduce consumption, for example through making their revenue from rentals of goods rather than sales.

Additional Impacts

Is your investment protecting habitat and livelihoods of endangered species?
Is your investment supporting companies that would not exist otherwise (often called "additionality")?

Innovation is a good benchmark to answer the question of how additional your investment is. As more innovative businesses and products tend to have a higher additionality, their approach is not prevalent in the market yet. However, they also tend to reduce emissions and pollution and therefore score higher in the environmental sustainability category.

Social Sustainability

The second pillar of sustainability is social impact. You want to ensure that your investments are supporting a shift in the social structures and helping those that are less well off. This might have the sound of charity, but it can make economic sense to invest in the less well-off.

Examples here would be:

- Solar systems on the roof of schools (clean energy and lower electricity bills)
- Providing a loan to a farmer to purchase equipment needed for harvest
- Energy efficiency measurements for a community building

The additionality principle is applicable here as well to ensure real social change is created.

Social sustainability can be an overlooked aspect of sustainability, as we could focus on environmental or economic sustainability. However, all three dimensions of sustainability must be addressed to attain the most sustainable outcome possible. An environmentally just world where only 1% are earning a living wage and have all the power will not create a thriving society and will not be long-term sustainable as inequality leads to conflicts and insecurity.

To get more clarity around this segment when you are making an investment decision, you can ask yourself any of the following questions. They are slightly wider and vaguer as social impact can vary.

Equity

Will your investment reduce in-equality?

This can be companies that have an active equality policy or that work with empowering people at the social margins. It can also be a women-led business or a business that focuses on working with and supporting women-led businesses and projects.

Diversity

Is your investment promoting diversity in terms of culture and ethnicity?

Again, this can be a core of the company/project you want to invest in or just something that they subscribe to as part of their work. It relates to the company's hiring policies, working conditions, the make-up of its leadership in terms of gender and race, if and how it shares its revenues with its employees, CEO vs worker salaries, to name a few.

Social Cohesion

Will your investment create or enhance a community and improve integration of that community in the larger society?

This could be companies that focus on education or invest in peripheral neighborhoods. Companies that want to spread education to under-served communities would be one example. This could for example be done through technologies used by some companies in East Africa, where they utilize digital classrooms to increase the number of students per teacher. Making education more affordable for the families of these students.

Life Quality

Will your investment improve the mental and physical health of a community and create opportunities for that group of people?

This could be companies working with handicapped people or investments in elderly homes that enhance the life quality of those sub-groups. It could also be companies developing new treatments for mental illnesses or just simple tools such as meditation techniques.

Employee Rights

Will your investment improve the working conditions of the employees? Will it allow people to earn a minimum wage that supports a decent life quality?

This could be companies that actively support fair payment in their company. This includes the right to unionize and to affect company policies and business practices. It is often hard to determine which companies have a positive agenda in this area, but one guideline could be certifications such as Certified B Corporations (which applies to several categories here).

Human Rights

Will your investment foster human rights and ensure fair treatment of any person involved in the company's business chain?

This concerns companies with unclear or vague value chains, for example in the clothing or food industry. You want to ensure that you ideally can follow the value chain of the company you are investing in and that the company you are supporting has human rights as a focus area of their operations.

Economic Sustainability

Finally, is the bottom line of all investing today: making money and a return on investment over time.

For an investment strategy to be sustainable economically it needs to make money in the long-term. As this is not intended to be for charity, your investments compete with the so-called opportunity costs of investing in other assets. And if one wants to move massive amounts of capital into the sustainable investing space, it needs to be commercially competitive.

Mind Your Money

This might seem slightly counterintuitive at first, as we tend to see profit as a bad thing and sort of at odds with a positive impact. However, the world we live in currently runs on capitalism and to make a big change we need to use that system for positive change.

We want projects and companies that are self-sustaining and do not rely on subsidies or donations to function. Much of the charity work has created unintended negative side effects due to a dependency on charitable money or organizations. We want to invest in companies that can grow sustainably through their own profits, so they can reach the scale they need to have a big impact.

Realistic Profit Expectations

Is the project you are investing in having a realistic profit expectation?

If not, it might jeopardize the other impact categories by, for example, over-charging customers or using cheap and unsustainable materials.

Not only returns are important, but we also want to ensure we do not lose our investments. Warren Buffet has a famous rule of investing:

> *"Rule No 1: Never lose money.*
> *Rule No 2. Never forget Rule No. 1."*

The reason for this is that whatever money you have lost, you will have to earn it back with the investments you have left. Which means that with many losses you will have to meet more and more unrealistic return targets to still earn money in the bigger picture.

For example, let's assume you have invested 100 EUR, and you want to make 110 EUR by investing it. Losing 50% of your investment suddenly raises the necessary return to reach the 110 EUR to levels extremely unlikely.

 Economic Sustainability

Original amount	Losses	Nominal target return	Necessary relative return
100	0	110	10%
100	50	110	120%

One way to avoid big losses is to bet on many different assets and diversify one's portfolio enough so that a down-turn in one asset class is covered by the increase of a different asset class (or at the very least not all your investments go down at the same time).

The balance between environmental, social, and economic impact is not easy. You will very unlikely find one investment that has a perfect balance on all three. But you can diversify your portfolio in such a way that you balance out these three segments overall.

I will explain more fully what I mean by diversification in Part III.

Economic Sustainability

III – How to Invest Sustainably?

So far, we have mainly covered theoretic ways of sustainable investing. However, the most important is of course to apply that knowledge to make a tangible difference.

Preparations

Pick a Good Financial Institution

You want to ensure that you save and invest your money via a good bank or community credit union. This is particularly important for your cash assets - if you decide to keep any. More on that later.

The money you deposit in a bank account is not just sitting there doing nothing, it is being used by the financial institution to create more capital and lend it out to borrowers. If these borrowers are not filtered according to a negative screening or a positive screening approach, you risk your money being used for causes that you do not want to support.

What are the criteria for identifying a sustainable bank? According to BankTrack it comes down to the following:[12]

Commitment to Sustainability
A commitment to sustainability forces banks to fully consider ecological limits, social equity and economic justice into corporate strategies and core business areas (including credit, investing, underwriting, and advising), to put sustainability objectives on an equal footing to shareholder maximization and client satisfaction, and to actively strive to finance transactions that promote sustainability.

Commitment to "Do No Harm"
Financial institutions should commit to do no harm by preventing and minimizing the environmentally and/or socially detrimental impacts of their portfolios and their operations.

Commitment to Responsibility
Financial institutions should bear full responsibility for the environmental and social impacts of their transactions.

Commitment to Accountability
Financial institutions must be accountable to their stakeholders, particularly those that are affected by the companies and activities they finance. Accountability means that stakeholders must have an influential voice in financial decisions that affect the quality of their environments and their lives -- both through ensuring that stakeholders' rights are protected by law, and through practices and procedures adopted by financial institutions themselves.

Commitment to Transparency
Financial institutions must be transparent to stakeholders, not only through robust, regular, and standardized disclosure, but also by being responsive to stakeholder needs for specialized information on financial institutions' policies, procedures, and transactions. Commercial confidentiality should not be used as an excuse to deny stakeholders information.

Commitment to Sustainable Markets and Governance
Financial institutions should ensure that markets are more capable of fostering sustainability by actively supporting public policy, regulatory and/or market mechanisms which facilitate sustainability and that foster the full cost accounting of social and environmental externalities.

To evaluate all these criteria in detail on a possible bank for your deposit might be a bit overwhelming. To simplify this further, I would suggest that at the very least the bank you are picking shows clear commitment to sustainability, responsibility, accountability, and transparency.

Sustainability is essential for picking a sustainable bank. It can be evaluated by the finance products the bank offers and generally how they position themselves.

Responsibility and accountability as they ensure the bank stays on course with its commitments. This is easiest fulfilled by picking a bank that is community owned and governed as that makes the bank accountable to more stakeholders than just big institutional investors.

Transparency as our new economic system is pushing towards a more transparent landscape, aided by the new technological advancements such as the internet. It is key for you to really be able to assess the banks' commitments in their actions.

As finding the right bank depends on where you are based, it is hard to give clear suggestions here. The easiest start is to search for banks that brand themselves as "ethical banks" or similar and then evaluate their words with their actions. One place that can make that search easier is the "Global Alliance for Banking on Values" which has members globally (including the ones below) and gives you a good starting point for your search.

GLS Bank (Germany)   **240,000 members**   https://gls.de

The GLS bank is one of the first ethical banks in Germany. The money of savers in GLS bank accounts is being used for loans to social and environmental impact-oriented companies. When you open an account, you can even pick what your money should be used for, anything from food, education, renewable energies, social and health and sustainable economy is possible.

Triodos Bank (EU)   **720,000 members**   https://triodos.com

Triodos is a Dutch bank with subsidiaries in many European countries, such as Belgium, Spain, United Kingdom, and Germany. It has pioneered a highly transparent model in which each project and company the bank invests in is listed on a special homepage (https://www.triodos.com/know-where-your-money-goes). They offer anything from a current account to a savings account and even investment funds.

**City First
(USA)** | **NA members** | https://cityfirstbank.com

City First is a bank focused primarily on social impact and supporting the under-served by ensuring that financial capital flows to impoverished neighborhoods. They provide savings and current accounts for private individuals as well as loans to businesses.

**Vancity
(Canada)** | **500,000+ members** | https://vancity.com

Vancity is a values-based financial co-operative serving the needs of communities in the Coast Salish and Kwakwaka'wakw territories, with branches in Metro Vancouver, the Fraser Valley, Victoria, Squamish, and Alert Bay. They offer anything from bank accounts, credit cards, mortgages, loans, insurance, and investments. Vancity does not invest capital or assets in oil, gas, or coal companies, nor do they provide investment banking services to facilitate access to capital for those companies.

**Cultura
Bank
(Norway)** | **NA members** | https://cultura.no

Cultura Bank's main task is to finance projects which benefit society and contribute to a better natural environment. The bank emphasizes building alliances between depositors and lenders and to underpin this it practices transparency as a carrying principle. It strives to offer high quality, solid banking services and be able to offer a healthy and sustainable return to shareholders.

<table>
<tr><td>Alternative Bank of Switzerland</td><td>35,000+ members</td><td>https://abs.ch/en</td></tr>
<tr><td colspan="3">ABS is a bank that focuses on social and environmental impact and offers anything from a savings account to ethical investment funds. They provide loans for social and ecological housing, organic agriculture, and renewable energy.</td></tr>
</table>

<table>
<tr><td>Ekobanken (Sweden)</td><td>2,000+ members</td><td>https://ekobanken.se</td></tr>
<tr><td colspan="3">Ekobanken is a member-owned bank that is committed to investments that are socially and environmentally sustainable. One a year they publish all the investments taken by the bank, therefore committing to transparency.</td></tr>
</table>

Set Up an Investment Account

First, you want to set up an account to invest with. This can be seen in different investment services at the same time, many of them being mentioned later in the book.

To do so, you often must pick an email address and go through a KYC process. If it is a more traditional bank account, you might even have to go to your bank to set up the investment account.

Set Your Investment Goals

Important before getting going is to be clear on why you are investing and what your goals are with your investments. Here are a few example goals that you could have:

- Retire early.
- Utilize your capital for impact.
- Make a return short-term.
- Save for your pension.

Depending on your goals you will have to make different investment decisions.

For example, if you want to make a retire early you will want to invest as much as possible every month and potentially pick higher return investment options. If you want to save for your pension however, you will likely be more conservative while still targeting investment opportunities that can give you a decent return.

Investing only to make a return in the short term, for example if you need the money soon, will make you want to pick minimal risk alternatives as you cannot bet on the market fluctuations that happen over decades. And of course, if you want to invest for impact or to be sustainable, you will potentially pick higher impact options with a higher risk.

Choose Your Investment Strategy

You need to be clear on how you want to invest and decide on an investment strategy. This heavily depends on your preferences in terms of risk and protecting your downside, partially linked to your goals.

My general suggestion is to establish a portfolio that is as diversified as possible. But if you want to focus on a certain asset class such as the most sustainable ones mentioned in this book, you can of course do that. Just keep in mind that you are taking a higher risk in terms of capital exposure which could result in losses that reduce the likelihood of a return. (On the other hand, there is the argument that if we do not invest in these assets that climate change will eventually decrease the value of all assets.)

We will discuss diversification in more detail in the Portfolio suggestions.

Start and Simplify

Once you have a plan in what you want to invest in, you will have to define how you want to invest in it. This includes everything from how often you want to invest to how you want to keep track of your investments and how to keep an eye on the balance of your portfolio. The general rule is that you want to keep it as simple as possible.

You want to make sure that you:

- Analyze your existing portfolio to see where you need to make changes
- Divest money from that part of your investments to more sustainable ones
- Have a clear plan on how to invest the divested (and any additional) capital
- Invest regularly in your decided investment strategy/portfolio

We'll cover these items and more in the coming section.

Analyze Your Portfolio

First off, it is important for you to have an overview of where you have your money invested. For some people this will be easy, for some not - it depends on how structured you already have your assets invested. This is a good moment to get more structured if you are not there yet.

Assuming you have capital locked in investments, the natural first step would be to look at your existing investments and analyze how sustainable those are. What you want to do is to see in which kind of assets your money is invested in, such as a cash savings account, real estate, stocks, government or corporate bonds, precious metals, or other alternative assets such as crypto currency.

You then want to calculate how much each of these assets represents the total invested capital. With a clearer overview and portfolio split you can then figure out how balanced your portfolio is according to the portfolio thinking laid out in the Economic Sustainability chapter and in the Portfolio suggestions section.

You will also want to assess which of your investments matches your own sustainability criteria (more on that later). By doing that you will be able to see how much you will have to divest and reinvest in sustainable assets instead.

Divesting

You most likely will realize that you either have a hard time fully understanding if the impact of your investments or that they are mainly negative. Not being able to understand the impact of your money in stocks, funds and other assets generally means that they are very likely not invested in a sustainable manner.

As you are reading this book, I take it for granted that you want to make your investments more sustainable and/or don't want to spend a lot of new capital on a new investment strategy. Therefore, you need to start looking at divesting some or all your invested capital.

To do so, you simply start selling assets that are liquid (easily sold) and that either can give you a return on investment while selling or at the very least give you a break-even on investment. As you want to avoid making losses when shifting assets, this is the preferred option. If you are fully committed to the impact investing paradigm you might divest your money, no matter the consequences. That is up to you and can be the right action for you. From an economic sustainability perspective, it is counterproductive though.

Once you have sold all the assets you wanted to liquidate, you have the capital to put in place in a new investment strategy.

Plan before divesting

You want to be sure you have a plan in what to invest your freed-up cash once you have divested. The longer you wait after selling assets and before investing in new ones, the more potential gains you are missing.

In the best scenario you already have identified specific assets that you want to invest in before you trigger the divestment process. In that way, you can shift directly over to your sustainable investments once you have the liquidity to do so. You should have decided which assets you want to invest in and how you want to split your portfolio amongst these assets. Make sure you have all accounts setup on the different service providers that you picked and that the only thing left is to send the cash earned through your divestment.

Do not over-think this step either as you can always make small tweaks to your portfolio, replace certain assets, and increase or decrease your exposure to them. The most important thing, as in many other parts of life, is to get going.

Investment Selection

How does one select the investments of one's portfolio? The next pages will dive more into how to assess your investment alternatives and decide on what you want to invest in.

Negative Screening

There are different ways to ensure that one uses the money to do go. You can either decide that you do **NOT** want to invest in certain sectors (negative screening) or that you **ONLY** want to invest in certain sectors (positive screening).

Negative screening, or exclusionary screening, is one of the most basic methods of separating socially responsible investments from those that are likely to have a negative effect on society. It is much less restrictive than positive screening as it only provides a blacklist of industry sectors and practices that do not align with the investor's intentions or values. These could include anything from companies that work in gambling or alcohol to companies that emit large amounts of greenhouse gases.

Negative screening is very widely adapted as it does not put too stringent requirements on an investment strategy. It mainly tries to prevent worst-case investments from happening, while all other cases are accepted. Therefore, it is rather manageable and easy to enforce.

However, the acceptance of so many cases is also its biggest disadvantage as it does not prefer companies with a big social impact over companies with hardly any positive impact (but no major negative impact either). Therefore, it does not foster major changes in our society to more sustainable practices as the companies left for this investment strategy are targeted also by other "normal investors". In a nutshell, it does not actively promote sustainable alternatives.

Here are some criteria it could a negative screening could utilize:

- Ethical issues, such as weapons trade, tobacco, pornography, alcohol production, gambling, and animal welfare
- Social issues; human rights and labor standards issues including health and safety, child labor, equal opportunities
- Environmental issues, such as pollution, climate change, transport, and resource management
- Governance issues, such as executive remuneration, board structure, bribery, and corruption

These negative screening criteria can vary widely between funds which leads to some funds seeming to be more sustainable than they really are. For example, some funds that are called ethical or sustainable allow companies in their portfolio even if up to 10/20% of their revenue or profit is coming from fossil fuels. Also, many companies with questionable business practices when it comes to working conditions are allowed in many such funds.

Positive Screening

Positive screening takes a different approach. It focuses on companies that are actively working towards a sustainable future, be it social or environmental. In this approach the goal is to identify these "sustainable leaders" in the market, while companies that are only working with the status-quo will not be considered for investment.

This investment strategy really intends to support companies that want to make a difference. Therefore, it not only invests in companies that are already having a positive impact, but it also encourages the industry to consider impact as a company target to receive investment. '

What are the typical positive screening criteria?

- Companies that produce innovative and sustainable products
- Companies with fair working conditions, worker participation in the decision-making process or even innovative business structures such as cooperatives
- Companies that apply innovative business models such as renting out equipment instead of selling it or enabling people to share resources with each other

Part of a positively screened investment portfolio may consist of start-ups that have come up with innovative products that enhance the world's sustainability. Examples are companies generating renewable energy, such as solar power, wind power, and hydrogen fuel cells; manufacturers of natural food and healthy living products; and companies involved in environmental clean-up and recycling.

Unlike negative screening, which generally is more black and white, positive screening requires an analysis of complex issues such as pollution, workplace practices, diversity, and product safety. This can be very restrictive and leave only a few companies and industry sectors to invest in. Which in turn can make it riskier due to the lack of diversification. It also takes more time to manage investments as the investor takes a slightly more active role in identifying these sustainable leaders in the market.

To achieve a well-diversified portfolio large and medium-sized companies are required. Larger companies generally tend to have more complex problems and are more complex to assess. Positive screening can help to assess which of these companies are heading in a positive direction. Bigger funds and institutions then often include a tobacco company that is showing leadership in its industry (is "best in class"), despite the overall record of that industry.

Maintain a Healthy Portfolio

The main guideline of traditional investing is to make sure your assets are future proof and sustain the test of time to create a financial return. The only difference in sustainable investing is that you also want to have the impact that you are aiming to achieve. Lost money is also lost opportunity for impact. In the end these two can be very similar.

Once you are set up with your initial portfolio you want to ensure that it stays healthy and balanced. To plan what you want to invest in, you will have to define how you want to invest in it. This includes everything from how often you want to invest to how you want to keep track of your investments and how to keep an eye on the balance of your portfolio. The general rule is that you want to keep it as simple as possible.

You want to make sure that you:

- Allocate your capital in a balanced way.
- Balance your portfolio regularly
- Track your investments and try to automate them as much as possible

We'll cover these items and more in the coming section.

Diversification

One of the most important rules is not to invest all your "eggs" into one "basket". The eggs here are your money and the basket can be anything from one industry sector, one geographic focus to one company or one asset class.

For example, many people mainly invest in stocks as they seem to have the best potential to increase in value and give returns. However, in this case you are over-exposed to only one asset class (being stocks) so if there is a market downturn you will lose a lot of value and violate the "Never lose money" rule.

To avoid this, you should think about your investments from a portfolio view and have an overview of what asset classes you have invested in. I will provide you with some suggestions on investment criteria, but generally you should split your capital into as many asset classes as possible if you want to achieve diversification.

Each of these asset classes reacts in their own ways to market changes, meaning if one asset loses in value, one or some of the others could gain in value and due to the diversification, the impact on your portfolio is balanced.

In addition to assets, you want to make sure to cover several geographic areas, by for instance investing in emerging markets such as Africa or Asia. These are areas that are partially non-correlated to European and American markets and therefore can provide you with a return while European investments stall or lose value. As there is still a lot of work to be done in these emerging markets, they also show higher return rates than more settled markets in Europe or North America.

The investment analyst Harry Browne has termed a type of a well-diversified portfolio as the "Permanent Portfolio." He looks at the market of a combination of four main market developments - rising and falling growth and inflation.

Throughout time and geographies, different asset classes have performed well in each of these four market environments. Therefore, all these assets make sense to invest in different market conditions. Ray Dalio, another famous investor, termed them seasons. We unfortunately cannot predict which season is coming next and when the change will happen. Sometimes several seasons could even occur at the same time! These surprises have an impact on asset prices due to unexpected changes in growth and inflation.

Considering this reality, a Permanent Portfolio contains four sub-portfolios - one for each economic environment containing assets known to perform well in that environment. The weights on the assets then need to be balanced to attain equal risk in each of the four environments. The diagram below shows the four economic environments containing examples of relevant asset types, with risk divided equally across environments.

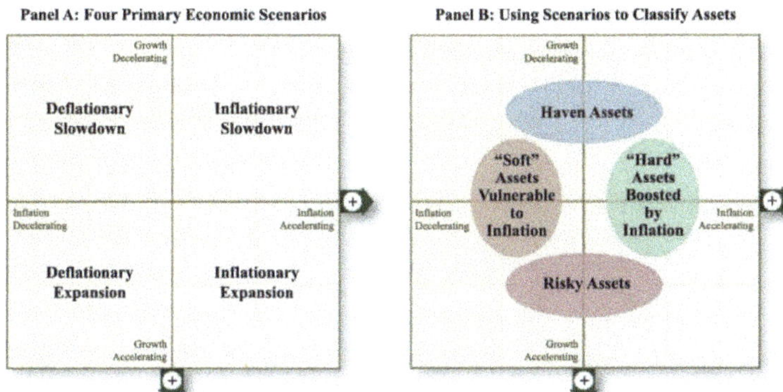

Figure 3 - The four economic environments containing examples of relevant asset types

The Permanent Portfolio investing mindset considers that we can't forecast the future and therefore don't know which growth/inflation conditions will unfold and when. As a result, it assigns weights such that there is an equal amount of risk (25%) in each of the 4 possible growth/inflation environments. This leads to the portfolio being able to perform no matter which growth/inflation environment eventuates.

However, an equal share of risk does not mean that you should invest equally in the assets in your portfolio. Rather, the total portfolio should react similarly to movements in the different scenarios. Equity therefore does not take the biggest role in the mix as it reacts rather volatilely to market developments.

The portfolio looks something like this:

- 25% Equity Risk
- 50% Bond Risk
- 25% long-term treasury bonds (20-25 years)
- 25% US intermediate-term treasury bonds (7-10 years)
- 25% Commodities Risk

Most of what is being suggested in this book can be categorized in these asset classes. You can of course build your own version and play around with the exposure to different assets, but generally you should aim to balance your portfolio according to the underlying risks.

Diversify to Keep Having an Impact

Diversification is not only a strategy to ensure a return on capital. It is also important to make an impact.

Putting all your assets in one asset class might have a big impact initially - if you invest it for example in reforestation or green start-ups. But you also risk losing all that capital in the short term after which you will not be able to make any future investments and therefore no more impact.

In that sense it might seem counter-intuitive, but diversifying your capital amongst different asset classes, some of them arguably less sustainable than others, could give you an upside in bad market conditions such as a recession or inflation period. When you then rebalance your capital, you will have to reinvest it in the assets that have reduced in value - in that case the higher impact ones. Doing so you provide additional capital to the more sustainable investments.

Additionality

One of the most important aspects to consider for sustainable investing is the additionality of your capital. Additionality refers to the actual effect of you choosing a certain investment opportunity.

If your investment has additionality, it means that it is invested in an asset that would not have been possible without it.

For example, if you decide to only use a negative screening approach, you will be picking investment cases that would be financed in any case and just leave out the ones that you really don't want to invest in. You are not doing anything in the market that has not already been done.

While with an approach of positive screening for example, you can decide that you want to invest in smaller companies that raise fresh capital through different means (more on that later). In such a case, your capital goes to a company or project that is actively seeking capital and might not be attractive for main-stream investors due to its niche focus, for example.

In the second case your capital has a clear additional effect, meaning that it supports innovation and impact that could not have been possible without it.

Best you always ask yourself *"How additional is my capital in this case?"*. This does not mean that you should not invest in assets that are not clearly additional, but for the portion of your portfolio that you want to be the most impactful, additionality can be key.

Investment Management

In the following page we will look deeper into how you should manage your investments.

Invest Regularly

There is no silver bullet in regular investing, but the more often the better. In the end it is a cost-benefit balance where you want to put yourself on the cadence of investing.

Reinvest after Your Rebalancing

To get started you could invest all the cash you have earmarked for investment at once. By doing so, you will be subject to a one-time price point of the asset you are buying. Many would believe that if you try to time the market with investing at the right moment, it is close to impossible to achieve a good result.

Given that one cannot time the market and tell whether it will go up and down, the best bet is to assume the average which is slightly positive. Therefore, if you have a large amount of capital ready to invest, the most rational decision is to invest it all directly. Waiting does not increase the chance of an up-market, instead it leaves you outside of the market and without the average gains. Empirical studies confirm that "lump sum investing" beats dollar cost averaging in about 65% of yearly horizons, and 85% of 5-year horizons.[13]

You will have to define for yourself what is your approach and what does not affect your mental health too much. If investing everything upfront is too risky in your view, you could invest about 50% of all your assets immediately (spread across your future portfolio) and the remaining 50% over a period of 6-12 months together with what you are committed to invest regularly.

Another possible strategy is to invest 20% of your assets every month over a 5-month period, together with what you are committed to investing in regularly.

As always with investing, there is no guarantee that either of these strategies will have a positive effect and protect you from losses.

Investing after Your Initial Reinvestment

For your on-going investments it is beneficial to invest regularly. How regular depends on how much time you want to spend managing this and on your financial situation. A good idea is to invest monthly and to automate as many of your investments as possible. Even investing quarterly is still a lot better and gives you 4 times the opportunity to "time" the market than if you invest once a year.

The idea here is that the more often you invest the better it is for the average price of your assets. As you will invest at times that have high prices and times with low prices you will be able to reach a good average price over time.

Automation

You should aim to automate as many of your investments as possible. This will open time and make you think less about your investments. The often cited "set it and forget it" mentality applies here. If it is automatic, you also will not be tempted as much to sell when prices are dropping or to buy more when prices are going up. You want to be as rational as possible when it comes to investing.

Some investments will likely not be able to be automated as not all investment services offer such a function. The best in such cases is to keep track of what you need to invest regularly in the place where you track your investments. This can be an Excel or Google Sheet that gives you an easy way to oversee all the different places where your assets are invested. With such tools you can automatically increase the portfolios that are being invested by the "robots" and have an overview of how much needs to be invested in the ones that are done by yourself.

In the case you cannot automate certain assets, you often can at the very least put the money aside. This can be done by, for example, setting up an automatic transfer to the account from where you are investing. By doing so you are not tempted to spend the money you have sitting in your regular bank account as it gets mentally allocated to another usage.

Some assets you cannot buy so easily in smaller tranches, for example government treasuries can be quite highly priced per bond note. In such cases sending your money to the accounts helps you keep
yourself accountable so you have the money available to invest in those assets once you can afford the higher ticket price.

Investment Tracking

To make having a plan and following it easier, I suggest you to setup a way to track all your different assets in one place. If you want to have a truly diversified portfolio and make an impact in different areas, you will have to spread your investments in quite a few different places. This is of course not ideal and takes time, so in the end it is up to you how you want to approach your investment strategy.

As you see in the later chapters in this book, once we get into tangible asset classes, they are available in many different places. So how to keep the overview? What I did is create one Google spreadsheet - yes very low-tech - where I track my existing investments. In a semi-automatic way, you can also keep track of your regular investments (if you decide to do so) by adding some simple formulas to the sheet.

You can split your Google Sheet into different tabs, each tab representing one asset class or one sub-portfolio. For instance, I do have tabs for most asset classes such as equity, real estate, debt and equity crowdfunding or real estate.

Of course, this really depends on your liking and taste. Generally, it is important to have a clear overview of your investment portfolio, even if you are not an investing big amount.

Portfolio Rebalancing

As part of your investment strategy, you want to make sure that you keep your portfolio balanced according to the criteria you have defined for yourself. Be that a strict Permanent Portfolio balance or a mixture. To achieve this, you should at least once a year examine the ratios of different assets in your portfolio and rebalance them.

Why do you have to do it in the first place? And how does one do that?

The why is simple. As different assets in your portfolio make major gains while others might make losses or stay stable, the portfolio split you started with starts to unbalance. Your emotional self might now want to put more money in the assets that are increasing in value, but rationally you should do the opposite. As if some of your assets lost value, you can now buy them cheaper than before. The only thing you must ensure is that your portfolio split is sensible and protects you from most downsides.

The how depends slightly, but the simplest way is to use the tracking of your investments I described in the chapter "Setup a way to track your investments ". This way you can see in one place what your portfolio should look like and can adjust according to how it looks. Here you make comparisons and define the difference in the asset classes.

Next, you can go about it in different ways, depending on your availability of capital.

If you have capital available to invest, you could just invest in the assets that are too low compared to where they should be according to their share of the portfolio. This can get rather costly if you have a sizable portfolio but is a good way to not have to sell valuable assets.

If you don't want to increase your exposure in your portfolio(s), then the easiest way is to sell a part of the assets that have increased in value and invest in the asset classes that have diminished in value. This can become slightly complicated to calculate as you are selling assets while you are reinvesting their value but should be doable (you can also check the example below). The advantage of doing this is that you materialize some of the value increase of your assets while you reinvest it cheaply in other parts of your portfolio. On the other hand, from a tax perspective it might not be ideal if you want to be a long-term investor.

Example of rebalancing while selling of some assets:

Asset	Target Value	Present Value	Re-balancing needed
Short-term bonds	100	100	0
Long-term bonds	100	90	+10
Gold	100	110	-10
Equities	100	120	-20

As you can see the first part seems simple: Short-term bonds don't require any adjustment, while Long-term bonds and gold can just be weighed against each other. However, the gain in stocks throws off the balance here.

The simplest trick here is to balance long-term bonds with gold so that all the first three assets have a value of 100. Then you must balance stocks to the portfolio. The first thing that might come to mind is to sell 20 and invest it in the rest, but then you have less in stocks than in the other assets.

What you want to maintain is the ratio between the asset classes. Which in this case is 25% each.

If you sell 20 in equities, all assets would be 100. However, you likely want to reinvest the money from selling the equities, which in that case you then would need to do equally amongst all assets, including equities. This would lead to an investment of 5 in each asset. The simpler way of handling this is therefore to just sell 15 in your stock asset class and invest 5 in each of the other 3 asset classes, making each asset worth 105 in the end.

This is a rather simple example and should only give you an idea of different possible scenarios. It can often look slightly more complicated; in which case it is often best to sell and buy assets until the asset allocation is according to your investment plan. After that you can invest any remaining unallocated capital according to your pre-defined split.

IV – What to Invest in?

Now that we've talked about what you need to look for in sustainable investments, how to get started, and why to diversify, it's time to look at how to evaluate and decide what investments to make.

There are many types of assets you could invest in. We will cover the most common and some innovative ones later the book, but we'll discuss some of them briefly in this section

Rating System

In the latter parts of this book, we will dive into specific asset classes and examples. This can be a great starting point, but in general I believe it is helpful to have a framework in mind that one can utilize when assessing any investment opportunity.

In this case we are going to use a simple rating system with which you can then compare investment opportunities that you have identified as being sustainable. This will enable you to make smarter decisions.

With so many very different asset classes, it is hard to compare them to each other. Therefore, we are using a basic rating system to assess the assets in 8 different areas. This is not a scientific method, but it provides you with a possibility to compare the various assets to each other. Note that some of the categories only show ⭐, ⭐⭐⭐ and ⭐⭐⭐⭐⭐ as they are a more basic criterion.

Liquidity

It is important to determine your time horizon before deciding what type of assets you should have in your portfolio. You might be relatively young with several decades of working and investing ahead of you. Or you might focus on the short-term if you are, for example, divesting your pension. This will result in a different time horizon for your investments.

Sustainable investing often means having a long-term horizon rather than only thinking short-term (trading stocks back and forth for example can hardly be sustainable).

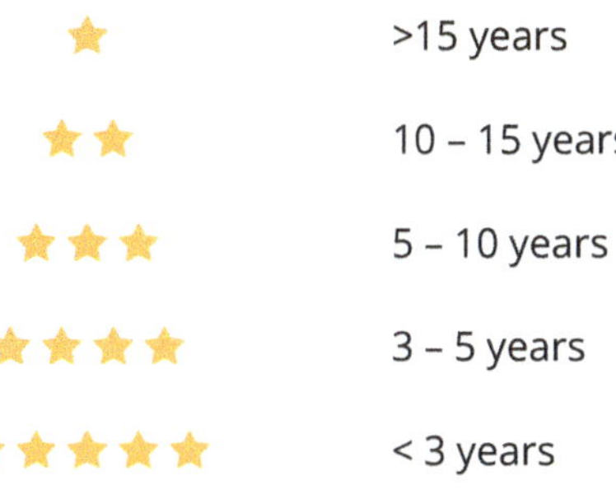

Additionality

Some of the assets mentioned later are not actively pursuing sustainability but are rather neutral in their impact. You can invest in these assets if you want to balance your portfolio, but they take money away from the more actively positive investments. Ideally, you want to make sure that what you are financing is additional. That means that it would not have happened without your financing.

For example, some carbon off-setting projects are being criticized in that they would have happened even without the carbon finance in place.[14]

 Negative additionality, investment in a negative industry

 No additional impact, investment in a neutral industry

 No additional impact, investment in a sustainable industry

 Positive additional impact, investment in an existing industry with product or business model innovation

 Positive additional impact, investment in a new and positive industry

Rating System

Environmental Impact

Not all assets mentioned will be environmentally positive and sustainable. You want to make sure that as much of your capital as possible is invested in environmentally sustainable assets, while also being comfortable with the level of risk you are taking. For the sake of simplicity, we will limit this rating to greenhouse gas emissions as they are often the easiest to assess.

 Negative with additional CO_2 emissions, e.g., fossil fuels

 Neutral with no CO_2 emissions, such as companies that make products that are carbon neutral

 Positive with negative CO_2 emissions, such as projects that remove CO_2 from the atmosphere

Social

A positive environmental impact is at the very least questionable if it is achieved with a negative social impact. For example, an authoritative country such as China might be more effective at combating climate change as they can easier impose limitations on their population. However, wanting every country in the world to replicate that model would come with a negative social impact that might not justify the environmental gains. Ideally, you want to invest in companies and assets that are both environmentally and socially positive.

Investment opportunity that has a negative social impact and actively degrades social rights

Investment opportunity that has a neutral social impact, meaning it is not a focus area of the underlying asset

Investment opportunity that has a positive social impact, meaning that it has a clear focus and goal on social issues

Transparency & Control

The majority of investing today is rather abstract and it is hard to understand what your money is really being used for. That might be fine if the overarching criteria are aligned with our values. You might prefer to know what you are investing in and the impact you are contributing towards.

 Very broad, no possibility to get clear view

 Very broad, rough breakdown of use possible

 Broad, but in specific (positive) industry or company

 Narrow, for example in a specific company within a specific use area, e.g., renewable energy

 Specific use of funds, for example in a specific project or for a specific product

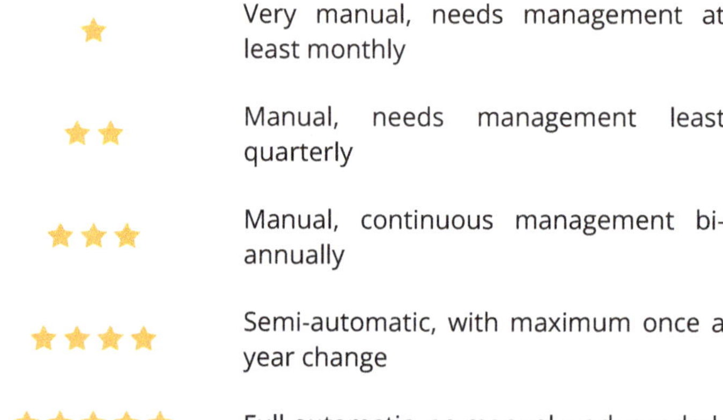

Time and Effort

Time is the scarcest resource in the world as it is truly non-renewable. You want to make sure that you decide well on how much time you want to spend on managing your portfolio of assets. Some of you might only want to go the automatic route of robo-advisors or professional wealth managers while others might enjoy the manual work of investing a lot and want to spend more time on it.

★	Very manual, needs management at least monthly
★★	Manual, needs management least quarterly
★★★	Manual, continuous management bi-annually
★★★★	Semi-automatic, with maximum once a year change
★★★★★	Full-automatic, no manual work needed

Risk

The above questions all sum up the bigger question of the risk that you are willing to take with your investments. More passive and more liquid investments with a high transparency can be less risky, while more additional investments can be riskier. This is highly generalized of course as each individual investment carries its own risk.

Nevertheless, you could argue that taking a higher risk in the short-term can be more sustainable, while in the long-run sustainable investments carry the lowest risk due to their resilience in terms of climate change.

Note, here less stars mean a riskier investment, therefore a lower rating.

Start-up, company, or asset class with no track record. Very volatile.

Established profitable company or hard assets such as real estate.

Asset with a lot of history and low risk of default or value destruction such as gold.

Return

An economic metric that cannot be ignored of course when talking about investments is the return. Not all sustainable investments are competitive with more traditional investment assets, and you need to find a balance that works for your investment strategy and goals. Of course, returns are not guaranteed and in some asset classes it also can vary widely depending on which sub-asset you invest in. Note, this might also shift in different countries and economic situations.

⭐	1 – 3 % p.a. above inflation
⭐⭐	3 – 5% p.a. above inflation
⭐⭐⭐	5 – 7% p.a. above inflation
⭐⭐⭐⭐	7 – 9% p.a. above inflation
⭐⭐⭐⭐⭐	>9% p.a. above inflation

  Rating System

Equity

Equity investing is basically purchasing stocks in companies to own a certain percentage of them, with the goal of either earning dividends or selling the stock to gain capital later. As an equity investor you also receive voting rights, which enable you to vote for candidates of the board of directors and even - if you hold a big enough share of the company - influence management decisions. Your capital invested can be used by the company to pay for its operation and therefore is a way of supporting industry players that you want to support and see succeeding.

Most equity can today easily be bought on the major stock exchanges when companies are publicly traded. Many early-stage companies are, however, privately owned and therefore harder to invest in. This is slowly becoming simpler though through other alternative routes such as crowdfunding where you can invest in early-stage start-ups.

Stocks can be divided into value and growth stocks. Value stocks have sizable cash flows in the present that stay stable or reduce over time. Growth stocks have little or no cash flow today, but are expected to increase them over time due to market adaption

Value stocks also often pay out dividends. The impact of high inflation often makes these stocks less attractive compared to during low inflation, due to dividends tending to not compensate for the inflation levels.

Equities perform well in a growth market with low inflation, but one can't generalize about inflation's impact on equities, as different groups of stocks seem to perform differently. In general value stocks perform better in high inflation periods and growth stocks perform better during low inflation. When inflation is on the upswing, income-oriented or high-dividend-paying stock prices generally decline.

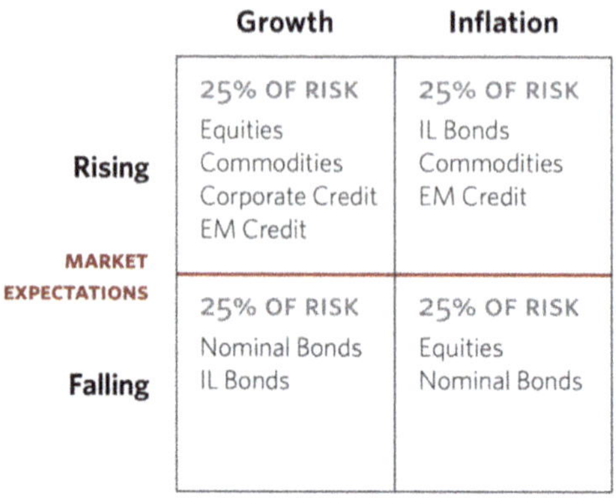

	Growth	**Inflation**
Rising	25% OF RISK Equities Commodities Corporate Credit EM Credit	25% OF RISK IL Bonds Commodities EM Credit
Falling	25% OF RISK Nominal Bonds IL Bonds	25% OF RISK Equities Nominal Bonds

MARKET EXPECTATIONS

Chart 1 - Equity Risk Profile

But stocks overall do seem to be more volatile during highly inflationary periods and therefore can be seen to perform best in general in rising growth and falling inflation scenarios.

Equity

Publicly Traded Stocks

Stocks in publicly traded companies have been around for a while and most of us are familiar with them. They are simple to buy and have a proven past return.

By investing in stocks, you own a percentage of the company you are buying the stocks from. You can then either get a return when the value of the company increases and you sell your ownership stake or through dividends, which is your share of profit of the company and is paid out regularly to all shareholders.

Environmental Impact

The environmental impact of stocks really depends on what you invest in as you have the freedom to choose and pick companies that fit your decision matrix. The most obvious advantage of investing in stocks is that you know where your money goes. You might not know exactly every detail of what the company is doing, but you still get more insight than, for example, investing in a fund.

It is often hard to fully understand a company's impact though as the world we live in is getting more complex with every day. So often you will have to make decisions with imperfect data and with accepting that there are probably quite a few things that you don't know about the industry or company that you are investing in.

Take as an example Tesla. Tesla clearly can have a very positive environmental footprint and is heralded by many to be a game changer for the environment. But it depends a lot on the business model Tesla chooses. Replacing all the cars we own in the world with electric cars will create another problem when it comes to resource extraction, of materials like Lithium for their batteries.

Tesla had the plan to offer a car sharing feature where people do not have to own cars but instead can order a pickup service like a taxi. It is hard to predict today if Tesla will decide to offer this service or just continue being another car manufacturer. This means that you are betting on a company strategy with the hope that it will not change in ways that reduce or even completely negate the positive impact of your investment.

This applies to most companies that you can buy stock of. Most existing companies need to change their business model to be a more sustainable enterprise. There are exceptions, such as investing in renewable energy companies. But most innovative companies with new business models are at too early a stage for you to be able to buy their stocks on the stock market. Thankfully there are other ways to invest in them nowadays which we get to later.

Social Impact

The social impact of stocks is like the environmental one. You must be smart in your choice of companies you decide to invest in to be positive.

Not all companies that have a positive environmental impact also have directly a positive social impact. Sometimes you could even argue the opposite. Take Tesla for example. They might in a perfect world with the right business model of driving as a service be a good environmental company. But the working conditions at Tesla factories have repeatedly been reported as non-humane or destructive to some - physically and psychologically. This clearly cannot have a positive social impact.

On the other hand, take United Natural Foods as an example. Not only are their products healthier and more sustainable than many competitors, they also actively try to have a positive impact on people's lives. Their employees are paid fairly, receive support in financially hard times, and can receive training and education. They also reduce their food waste by donating most of it to charities and are actively committed to racial equality of their staff. Which is a lot more than most other food retailers are even considering doing.

What you want to look out for are companies that have socially responsible ingrained in their values and have a track record to show. They should actively offer transparency around their business practices and clear objectives or strategies on how they aim to achieve social sustainability.

                    Equity

Economic Impact

From an economic perspective, one advantage of stocks is that you don't have to pay any fees to a fund manager or similar as you are the one picking the stocks. This can seem little on an annual basis (0.5 - 1.5% p.a.) but it adds up over time. There might be trading fees via the stockbroker you are using, but if you are a long-term investor and do not plan to trade stocks frequently these costs are minor nowadays.

Stocks are also a highly liquid asset, meaning that you can sell them rather quickly while not incurring big fees when selling. This does not imply that you can sell them fast at any price of your liking, but you can liquidate them instantly during the opening hours of the stock exchange if you price them at or below the current market value.

Historically, stocks have had about 8% return per year. If you diversify your portfolio into different geographies and industries, you can potentially expect similar returns over the long run.

However, you do have to manage your investment actively. Depending on the level of insight you want, you might want to do in-depth research about the companies you are picking. You might want to understand each companies' business and business model to truly be able to assess how they make their money and how sustainable they are.

You also will have to rebalance your stocks on an even more detailed level than, for example, with funds. Assuming you spread your capital amongst many stocks, the redistribution of capital from stocks that perform to those that are not performing can become quite tedious. You end up doing the job of a fund manager and depending on your interest you might want to spend your time on other things and pay the fee for such funds.

Equity

Rating

Liquidity

Stocks are one of the most liquid assets that you can buy. You can sell them at any time if there is a buyer.

Additionality

Buying stocks does not have the highest additionality. You can of course buy stock of companies you deem sustainable. But the capital you use to buy the stock does not go to the company and its operations, but rather to its shareholders from which you buy the stock.

Environment

There are options that can have a positive impact. As the additionality is compromised, this asset class is rated between neutral and net positive.

Social

There are options that can have a positive impact. As the additionality is compromised, this asset class is rated between neutral and net positive.

Transparency

You do have some control over where your money goes and which industry you support. But in the end, as your money does also not go directly to the company nor a specific project, it is not the highest it could be.

Effort

Buying stocks is easier than it has been previously. But as you need to balance your equity stakes in the different companies and in your overall portfolio, it requires more time and effort from your end than investing in alternatives discussed later.

Risk

Stocks are most often invested in established companies and compared to other investment assets in this book are less risky. That does not mean that you could not lose your capital, but depending on the company whose stock you buy, this can often be relatively low risk.

Return

Over long-time public stocks have shown an average of 8% p.a. return.

Practical Examples

You could use one of the many sustainability rankings of companies out there to identify the most sustainable ones. However, these lists often focus on existing market players and include companies whose sustainability can be argued about. Such as the likes of H&M, Nestle or even oil companies.

So best is to focus on sectors that are more sustainable and try to pick sustainability leaders in those sectors.

Sustainable energy
As we need to shift to an economy based on renewable energy, this one is a no-brainer. Some examples are:

Tesla	TSLA	A solar installer and car manufacturer.	USA
Solar Edge	SEDG	A solar electricity provider.	Israel
Minesto	MINEST	An innovative wave electricity producer.	Sweden
SunPower	SPWR	A solar electricity producer.	USA
First Solar	FSLR	A global leader of photovoltaic solar solutions	USA
NextEra Energy	NEE	A global leader of energy output from solar and wind sources	USA
Scatec Solar	SCATC	An integrated solar power producer.	Norway

Equity

Sustainable transportation

Transportation being one of our major emission sectors, there is a clear need to enable this industry to become more sustainable. This can be done by either replacing fossil fuel cars with alternatives such as electric cars or new business models such as sharing cars instead of owning them.

Tesla	TSLA	A pioneer in electric cars	USA
Lyft	LYFT	Company promoting car sharing.	USA

You could also buy into the value chain of electric car manufacturers, such as Panasonic (one of the world's largest battery manufacturers), Albelmarle (one of the world's largest lithium mining companies) or automotive component producers such as Aptiv. However, the sustainability of the electric car industry is questionable to some extent as it has a huge environmental footprint. In the sustainable transportation segment, the jury is still out what makes sense to invest in. The best is to try to invest in companies that challenge the status quo of owning cars vs replacing one type of car with another type.

Special mention - NAI index

The "Natur-Aktien-Index" is a list of stocks that fulfil certain criteria of sustainable investing. It is not an index fund as such and rather lists stocks that you must choose and buy yourself.

The list uses in a first instance a negative screening method, removing any stocks that operate in the nuclear energy, arms production, discrimination of women and ethnic minorities, child labor, testing on animals, genetically modified agriculture, and production of environmental or health-damaging products.

The companies on the list also must fulfil at the very least two of the following four positive screening criteria:

Mind Your Money

1. They offer products or services that provide solutions to environmental and social issues of humanity, such as:

    - Renewable energy production
    - Organic agriculture
    - Efficient water technology
    - Social and environmentally oriented research, financing, and consulting
    - Poverty alleviation

2. They are market leader in their industry regarding their product innovation:

    - Lifespan and efficiency
    - Product safety
    - Recyclability
    - Replacement of dangerous substances

3. They are market leader in their industry regarding the technical implementation of their production processes such as:

    - Reduction of energy and resource consumption
    - Environmental compatibility as a core of their business
    - Continuous improvement of their environmental performance

4. They are market leader in their industry regarding the social impact of their production processes such as:

    - Creation of jobs
    - Security and health protection in the workplace
    - Above average availability of further education of their work force
    - Special social benefits
    - Support of women, social and ethnic minorities

                              Equity

The NAI itself consists of stocks that:

- Are spread amongst a diverse set of industries and geographies
- At least 75% of the stocks in the NAI from of companies earning more than 100 million EUR revenues per year
- Up to 25% of the stocks in the NAI are from companies that develop innovative products which have not yet reached 100 million EUR revenues per year.
- Are deemed to be profitable in the long-term

The NAI should show a long-term trend and be comparable with other international stock indexes. Furthermore, it must be provable that the companies fulfil the criteria set out above.

Stocks will be removed from the NAI if:

- The environmental and social criteria are not met any longer
- The trading of these stocks is put on hold
- There is need to make room for more innovative and profitable companies in the NAI

One the next page is the list of actual stocks on the NAI as of November 2023.

Company	Country	Industry	ISIN-Nr.
Aixtron	Germany	Semiconductors	DE000A0WMPJ6
Aspen Pharmacare	South-Africa	Pharmaceutical	ZAE000066692
Biontech	Germany	Pharmaceutical	US09075V1026
East Japan Railway	Japan	Railways	JP3783600004
First Solar, Inc	USA	Renewable Energy	US3364331070
Interface	USA	Floor coverings	US4586653044
Kadant	USA	Paper recycling	US48282T1043
Kingfisher	GB	Home improvement stores	GB0033195214
Kurita Water Industries	Japan	Water management	JP3270000007
Li-Cycle	Canada	Battery Recycling	
Mayr-Melnhof Karton	Austria	Packaging	AT0000938204
Molina Healthcare	USA	Health Insurance	US60855R1005
Natura & Co	Brazil	Cosmetics	BRNTCOACNOR5
NVIDIA	USA	Semi-conductors, AI	US67066G1040
Ormat Technologies	USA	Geothermal Energy	US6866881021
Pearson	UK	Education	GB0006776081
Potlatch	USA	Wood products	US7376301039
Ricoh	Japan	Office machines	JP3973400009
Scatec	Norway	Renewable Energy	NO0010715139
Signify NV	The Netherlands	Light systems	NL0011821392
Sims Metal Man.	Australia	Recycling	AU000000SGM7
Smith & Nephew	GB	Medical technology	GB0009223206
Steelcase	USA	Furniture	US8581552036

Steico	Germany	Insulation Materials	DE000A0LR936
Svenska Cellulosa	Sweden	Paper	SE0000112724
Tesla Motors	USA	Electric Cars / Batteries	US88160R1014
Tomra Systems	Norway	Returnable Bottles Machines	NO0005668905
Umweltbank AG	Germany	Financial Sector	DE0005570808
United Natural Foods	USA	Ecological Food	US9111631035
Vestas Wind	Denmark	Wind Turbines	DK0010268606

While the companies on the list above vary in their sustainability and potential importance for humanity (cosmetics vs energy) this is a good list to start and pick several companies whose stock you wish to invest in. Looking at the criteria behind the NAI and the list of companies above you might also get a good feeling for how you could pick further stocks yourself.

Index Funds

Instead of investing in separate stocks yourself, you could simply choose to invest in a fund - in this example an index fund. Index funds are designed to follow certain rules depending on the fund structure. The goal is that the fund tracks a basket of underlying assets, such as following market indexes such as the S&P 500 or the Dow Jones.

These funds make up a big part (20%+) of all equity mutual funds in the US and other countries and have been adapted for various reasons.

Environmental and Social Impact

Let us talk about the elephant in the room. Index funds often follow the most well-established sectors. Which in the case of our current economy are most often unfortunately also the least sustainable sectors and companies. Couple this with the inherent non-transparency of such funds and you get an investment that can hardly be truly sustainable. There are potential exceptions to this, and we will talk about them later.

The environmental and social impact of index funds depends on what index funds you decide to invest in. The funds you choose should fit your investment criteria and have as stringent requirements as possible. However, index funds are broad on purpose which results in it being hard to truly understand what the fund is investing in. This makes them not the ideal asset if your aim is to invest as sustainably as possible with your investments.

What you want to ensure is that the fund restricts their investment solely to sustainable alternatives and has no loopholes that allow them to invest otherwise. You should check the companies they currently invest in as that gives you a good idea of what they might invest in going forward.

It must be noted that index funds are not a perfect fit for a sustainable portfolio as they are by nature passive. The advantage of low fees can only be provided due to this passive nature of index funds. But by doing so, index funds cannot employ an active screening method as doing so requires resources and time. At the best, they apply a negative screening method - which as we learned earlier has a lot of potential loopholes and disadvantages. The more sustainable you want your portfolio to be, the less index funds you should invest in due to their focus on a general market.

Economic Impact

Purely economically speaking index funds are a pretty good choice.

Most index funds have low fees, often below 0.5% p.a. Due to their design of tracking an index, investments within the fund rarely change, so there's little work for portfolio managers to charge you for, which makes them attractive from an economic perspective. If you invest $10,000 in an index fund with a 0.1% fee, you will pay only $10 per year, versus the $100 you'd owe annually if you invested in an actively managed fund with a 1% fee. And these fees will add up over time.

Not only do they have low fees. They also have competitive returns. Even the smartest portfolio managers cannot beat most index funds. Only a bit above 20% of actively managed funds generate a higher return than index funds - while having higher costs as well. You not only get higher returns, but you also pay less for those higher returns.
Index funds reduce your time spent on picking stocks and diversifying your portfolio. As they follow a certain pre-set rule you can invest an up-front amount and/or make regular investments in many different stocks. This aspect makes them a rather hands-off and simple investment asset.

Related to the time saving, index funds also provide immediate diversification. Indexes that track the S&P 500 for example spread your capital amongst 500 different investments. This diversification acts as a risk and volatility reduction.

Index funds follow simple rules which make them hands-off for investors. The downside of this is that you have little control over where your money is going. Even from the perspective of diversification, you could have the knowledge that certain companies in an index are overvalued, but you do not have the ability to act on that knowledge and decrease your exposure to these companies. There is also no guarantee that the fund will be following the chosen index 100% of the time as there is a possibility of tracking errors. In such cases you might lose or make money compared to the market index.

Rating

Liquidity

Index funds are one of the most liquid assets that you can buy. You can sell them at any time if there is a buyer.

Additionality

Index funds do not specifically follow a certain sustainability criterion, but rather try to follow an index as closely as possible. As they are also managed passively, they do not employ active screening methods.

Environment

Index funds often follow a market index and therefore their impact is like the general market. Even if the fund has a sustainable focus, their investments often are in companies not driving a huge impact, e.g., tech giants or banks.

Social

Like the environmental impact, index funds do not necessarily bring with them tremendous social change and justice.

Transparency

You have mainly control of what index you want to pick. There is a level of transparency in terms of what the index fund wants to focus on, but as this is a passive investment instrument, your control is limited.

Effort

Buying index funds or funds in general is a lot easier than previously. Compared to stocks, you only need to balance a few index funds. Therefore, it is one of the assets that requires the least time and effort from your end.

Risk

Index funds are one of the least risky investments as they follow the general indices of the market. If an index fund loses value, generally the segment of the market that the fund tried to follow also loses value. That does not mean that you could not lose your capital, but depending on the company whose stock you buy, this can often be relatively low risk.

Return

As they invest in stocks, index funds show a similar return over long time horizons with an average of an 8% p.a. return.

Practical Examples

Below are some funds that aim at offering sustainable index funds.

Öhman Etisk Emerging Markets A (Sweden)   Fee: 0.40%

An index fund that invests in emerging markets with a sustainable focus. The fund uses positive screening and sustainability aspects are crucial to the choice of company they invest in. Companies financed through the fund can however still gain up to 10% of their revenue through the fossil fuel industry.
The fund however has a lot of holdings in Chinese companies, which can be seen as highly doubtful sustainable assets due to their impact on the climate.

Öhman Global Marknad Hållbar A (Sweden)   Fee: 0.40%

An index fund that invests in global markets with a sustainable focus. The fund uses positive screening and sustainability aspects are crucial to the choice of company they invest in. Companies financed through the fund can however still gain up to 10% of their revenue through the fossil fuel industry.
The fund has more than 50% in American tech companies and financial institutions such as Visa.

First Trust ISE Global Wind Energy Index Fund   Fee: 0.62%
(FAN)

FAN tracks the ISE Global Wind Energy Index, an index following the performance of companies focusing on the wind energy industry.

The fund includes both wind power companies as well as companies that have a broader business model of which a part is focusing on wind power. It uses a blended strategy, investing in a mix of growth and value stocks of the wind energy sector in developed markets. Its biggest investments are in Siemens Gamesa, a Spain based provider of renewable energy services, Vestas Wind Systems, a manufacturer of wind plants in Denmark and Orsted, a renewable energy firm from Denmark.

---

iShares MSCI Global Impact ETF (SDG)   Fee: 0.49%

SDG follows the MSCI ACWI Sustainable Impact Index, which focuses on companies that generate at least half of their revenues from products and services that solve environmental and social challenges. It excludes companies that fail to meet minimum ESG standards. The fund's main target is large-cap companies from developed markets. To do so it employs a blended strategy of investing in both growth and value stocks. The fund's biggest investments are in Tesla, an electric car manufacturer and renewable energy company, NIO, an electric car manufacturer from China, and Vestas Wind Systems.

iShares MSCI Denmark ETF (EDEN)   Fee: 0.53%

EDEN tracks the MSCI Denmark IMI 25/50 Index, which focuses on the Denmark's equity market. The index contains 45 assets and covers about most of the free float-adjusted market cap of the Danish equity market. Similarly, the fund holds a total of 45 separate investments from the Danish equity market. It is not exclusively focused on ESG stocks, but still has an AAA MSCI ESG Rating and a MSCI ESG Quality Score of 9 out of a possible 10.
The fund's biggest investments include Novo Nordisk, a Danish pharmaceutical company, DSV Panalpina, a transport and logistics company, and Orsted.

Actively Managed Funds

The environmental and social impact of active funds depends - you guessed it - on what your fund invests in. Active funds are a better fit for a sustainable portfolio as they have educated investment managers that pick investments on your behalf based on the agreed upon criteria. Important for this to be relevant is that the fund uses an active screening method to select possible investments. By doing so you benefit from the active management of the fund in terms of increased sustainability.

Due to their active management style these funds can use a positive screening method, which allows them to find investment opportunities that are more sustainable than the market benchmark. This also means that they can be additional by providing capital to market leaders in the sustainability field.

It is important to not get "tricked" by fancy names. Many funds might have "ethical" or "sustainable" in their name, but you really need to look underneath the hood to see how strong these values are integrated in the fund. You might be surprised when you analyze some funds and see that some of them were not strictly following the sustainable investing mandate, but rather have it as a nice to have. Often, they can have exceptions to invest in companies that earn revenue from fossil fuels, if this revenue is not higher than a certain percentage. Often ethical funds also invest in companies such as Nestle or H&M which are at the very best questionable in their ethical practices and which have business models that are not aligned with a sustainable future with reduced consumption.

What you want to ensure is that the fund's restrictions for their investments are aligned with your values and focus on sustainable alternatives without possible loopholes that allow them to invest otherwise. You should check their investment portfolio and the companies they currently are invested in as that gives you an idea what the fund might invest in the future. If you find companies that you do not believe should be in a sustainable fund, avoid investing in that fund.

You often can find this information on the fund's data sheet under sections such as selection criteria. You will also find the assets under management on such a sheet, which shows you the top investments taken by the fund.

At the other end of the spectrum are actively managed funds which are - as the name suggests - actively picking the equity investments that match their investment strategy. These funds have therefore one or several fund managers which are rebalancing the portfolio and assessing new potential investment strategies. Generally, actively managed funds are more aligned with a sustainable fund portfolio, as they are less focused on the status quo of the market.

Environmental Impact

The funds that you invest in should have clear rules ensuring that they are not investing in companies that create part of their revenue with fossil fuels. This is important as there are numerous funds out that claim to be sustainable while still allowing companies that make a small share of their revenue with fossil fuels to be part of their investment portfolio. To be sure that this is the case you will have to take a detailed look at the investment strategy of the fund and what their rules are.

The best idea is also to invest in funds that have a positive screening approach. This ensures that they focus on market leaders or innovations rather than companies that often index funds cover as well as part of their investment strategy.

Social Impact

The social impact of active funds depends on the fund's investment criteria and screening methods. In the end this is like the impact of stocks as most active funds focus on stocks of companies matching their criteria.

Many sustainable funds are still investing in companies such as Amazon, whose social impact can at the very least be questionable, more realistically quite simply negative.

What you want to look out for are funds that have social screening criteria built into their investment process and preferably have a clear investment focus that includes social impact. Thematically focused funds are easier to assess in their impact focus than more general sustainable investment funds as they have a clearly defined investment mandate.

Economic Impact

Actively managed funds have higher fees than index funds, which reduces their potential economic return. Since they are actively managed, they do have to employ investment managers and alike to keep the fund operating. These fees can often be above 1%, which is charged no matter if the fund is profitable or not. As mentioned before, these fees add up over time.

They do reduce your time spent on picking stocks and diversifying your portfolio. As they follow a certain pre-set rule you can invest an up-front amount and/or make regular investments in many different stocks. This aspect makes them a rather hands-off and simple investment asset. Your capital is diversified in numerous investments when you decide to invest in an active fund. This ensures that it is very difficult or close to impossible to lose the full value of your investment.

As index funds, actively managed funds do make all the investment decisions in the fund. You have little control over where your money is going, besides the general focus of the fund. This can mean that the fund invests in industries that are slightly misaligned with your focus. Related to the lack of control, investing via actively managed funds is often not very transparent. There are exceptions to the rule, but generally you must trust the fund to be making investment decisions that are aligned with your values.

Rating

Liquidity

As with any fund, actively managed funds are highly liquid assets. You can sell them at any time if there is a buyer.

Additionality

Active funds employ active screening methods. By doing so, they can ensure that your money does good.

Environment

The right active fund can ensure that your capital is being put to good use and has a positive environmental impact. Due to the lower additionality this still is not a 100% rating though.

Social

Funds with the right screening methods can ensure that your capital is being put to good use and has a positive social impact. Due to the lower additionality, it is only 4 stars though.

Transparency

Investing in actively managed funds does give you more control over where your money goes as they themselves enact stricter rules on what to invest in. If those rules are in line with your investment strategy, you have a good control over your capital.

Effort

Buying funds in general is easier than previously. Compared to stocks, you only need to balance a few funds. Therefore, it is one of the assets that requires the least time and effort.

Risk

Active funds are slightly riskier than index funds as a fund manager makes decisions over what to invest in. That means they can underperform compared to the market. They do however spread the risk of your investment into many assets, which gives you a good diversification of your capital.

Return

Active funds are most of the time not outperforming the market and therefore on par with the other equity options discussed so far. Be aware of the often-higher fees though that can eat into your return. Due to these higher fees active funds are slightly downgraded in their rating here.

Practical Examples

Unfortunately, it is hard to give a full overview or understanding of how to find sustainable funds. It requires a lot of research and Googling. With the aim of giving, you a broad overview of several sustainable funds, here is a list of examples in different regions.

Handelsbanken Hållbar Energi (Sweden)   Fee: 1.5%

A fund that globally invests in companies that develop technologies (mainly renewable energy) to minimize the impact of global warming.

CB Save Earth Fund (Sweden)   Fee: 1%

A fund that invests in stocks of companies that actively work in renewable energy, water supply, clean tech, and other related industries.

Nanuk New World Fund (Australia)   Fee: 1.2%

The Nanuk New World Fund is a long-only equity fund that invests in listed companies exposed to the broad theme of environmental sustainability and resource efficiency. The Fund invests globally in companies involved in the areas of clean energy, energy efficiency, industrial efficiency, waste management, pollution control, food & agriculture, advanced & sustainable materials, water, and healthcare technology.

Domini Sustainable Solutions (USA)   Fee: 1.4%

A globally diversified equity portfolio that plans to keep its holdings to fewer than 50 and limit turnover. It will look for companies with strong ESG credentials that are developing products and services that are helping address the SDGs. Examples include renewable energy, electric vehicles, new medical technologies, healthy food, and financials that support underserved communities.

Triodos Pioneer Impact Fund (EU)   Fee: 1.8%

Triodos Pioneer Impact Fund aims to generate positive impact and competitive financial returns from a concentrated portfolio of small- and mid-cap companies pioneering the transition to a sustainable society. This is a relative high-risk fund as it invests in early-stage companies but has a potential of a high return.

Triodos Global Equities Impact Fund (EU)   Fee: 1.6%

Triodos Global Equities Impact Fund aims to generate positive impact and competitive returns from a concentrated portfolio of equities issued by large-cap companies offering sustainable solutions.

Triodos Energy Transition Europe Fund (EU)   Fee: 1.95%

The fund invests in wind farms, solar photovoltaic and solar thermal installations across Europe. Typically, these installations are privately owned and/or operated by a special-purpose vehicle. The fund invests through equity but also through debt investments.

Privately Listed Stocks

Private-listed stocks are shares sold by companies not trading on an official stock exchange (yet). Instead, they raise funds through tools such as equity crowdfunding.

Equity crowdfunding is a relatively new phenomenon. It is fairly similar to buying stocks on a stock exchange, with the main difference being that through equity crowdfunding you can invest in young start-up companies that are not yet publicly trading. This is something that previously was only available to sophisticated investors such as venture capital funds or angel investors which could invest bigger amounts of money. Due to its low entrance investment amounts, equity crowdfunding in contrast is accessible to most people that are investing some of their income.

There is clearly a higher risk in investing in early start-ups, however the upside is also bigger than compared to traditional publicly traded stock companies. For a younger investor putting some money aside for these high-risk assets makes sense due to the possible high return in the medium-term and their clear sustainability impact (if chosen wisely).

You should diversify your investments - even more so with early-stage equity funding. Which is why you should be mindful about your investments in this very early-stage equity investment.

Environmental Impact

While one could argue that the companies on the public stock market are in general not moving the needle much on status quo of sustainability, the start-ups raising capital in this way are often having the most innovative business models and products, also in terms of sustainability. You support an active change in our economy due to providing capital to these change agents.

Without your support the start-up would have to seek finance in other places, which can prove to be more difficult and less successful. Therefore, your action is not only sustainable, but also highly likely to create additional impact. Your investment and the start-ups you support can have true ripple effects in the economy that also nudges other entrenched market players to follow-suit and adopt similar practices to stay relevant.

The environmental impact of investing in start-ups depends on what kind of companies and on which platform you decide to invest. It is complex to give a furrow overview, but I will try to give some simple examples below of companies that can be seen as a positive investment.

You want to ensure that the company you invest in is tackling a problem related to climate change or sustainability in general. This can be either by providing a product that is made with sustainable materials, has a longer lifetime, or simply replaces existing products that are unsustainable. Best case it also has a sustainable business model that is not based on profiting from consumption, but rather profits from creating a closed loop or a more effective use of existing resources such as a subscription model or similar.

As you know exactly which company you are supporting it is a rather tangible and transparent asset class as you often get detailed insights into the company's operations.

Social Impact

You also should be as certain as possible that the start-up you are financing is actively working against any negative social impact, be it gender equality or poverty. The advantage with start-ups is that you can pick companies that are highly innovative in this field. Not all start-ups that are strong on the environmental impact side contribute to a strong social change.

However, often these two go together as the mind-set needed to go and start a company that is environmentally positive is very similar to the one needed to make a social impact.

In some cases, it is relatively clear that a company wants to bring social justice and equality to its market. If the product or service, the company sells has that element built in. This would be the case if you invest in a start-up that wants to innovate education and bring it to non-privileged parts of society. The company could also mention that it plans to pay its employees fairly or have a gender-balanced leadership.

In other cases, it is not as clear, and you need to either trust that the company will aim to minimize any negative social impact on society and that the environmental commitment already makes the company more conscious about social issues or you need to pick another investment opportunity instead.

Economic Impact

Start-ups are a high risk, high reward investment. As you are acting as an early-stage investor you can make high returns if the start-up is successful. However, most of the companies you invest in will likely fail as 9 out of 10 start-ups don't make it. This highlights the need for diversification even more. You will likely want to invest in a few dozen companies to ensure that the few that succeed will off-set the losses of the others. At the end of the day one good method is to keep your overall exposure to a level that you are comfortable losing completely in a worst-case scenario.

Hence why these investments are more time-intensive than others. You need to actively find investment opportunities that fit your investment criteria, often on different websites, in different currencies and with different levels of detail. You then need to either do a more thorough assessment of the business case or just invest in companies whose values align with yours and whose product or service you would buy yourself. Depending on your portfolio size and how much you are willing to invest in early-stage start-ups this might be too much considering your everyday responsibilities.

The advantage is that you do have ultimate decision power on where your money is invested and what it does support in the economy. With early-stage companies, there could be a change of the chosen business plan. As a shareholder you often get regular updates on business progress and get relatively deep insights into the workings of the start-up. If they do change course, you sometimes do have the chance to sell your shares on second-hand markets.

Equity

Rating

Liquidity

As with any fund, actively managed funds are highly liquid assets. You can sell them at any time if there is a buyer.

Additionality

Investing in start-ups and unlisted companies often means that you invest in an innovation that has potential to bring change on a massive scale. Your capital will most of the time also go directly to the company instead of its shareholders.

Environment

Like other investments, it depends on what companies you invest in. But as start-ups often are bringing in innovations, they can have a tremendous environmental impact.

Social

Here it also depends on what companies you invest in. There might be less investment opportunities that are socially impactful, but generally their potential is tremendous.

Transparency

Part of your investment is often a clear description of what your funds are intended for and what the company plans to do in the coming 6-18 months.

Effort

Investing via crowdfunding platforms can quickly take a lot of your time as the investment process has several steps and is not as straight-forward as most other ways of investing. Managing a portfolio of crowd investments can be a challenge.

Risk

Investing in early-stage companies comes with a high risk, high reward. These companies often have not proven their business model, nor are they cash flow positive.

Return

Investing in early-stage companies comes with a high risk, high reward. Most will fail, but the ones that are successful can be valued at a multiple of what they were worth when you invested in them.

Practical Examples

Equity in start-up stocks is available via investment platforms such as the below. They often do not differentiate much between each other, but you will have to go through an on-boarding process on each of them. To get started, you might want to test a few instead of creating accounts on all of them. To help you choose here is an overview of the most common ones.

Seedrs (UK)   **2 billion GBP invested**   seedrs.com

Seedrs is a "traditional" equity platform. You can pick the company you want to invest in yourself, or you can setup an auto-investment function that picks companies according to your preferences, such as sectors and number of investors. They frequently have sustainable companies on the platform, such as the previously mentioned Sustainable Accelerator, Sono Motors (shared electric car company), and fairafric (fairly traded chocolate that is produced in Africa with renewable energy).

You can also sell your shares in companies on Seedrs on a secondary market later. This is a bit unique as not all platforms over this kind of feature. It means you don't have to wait for an IPO of a start-up or any other exit event, but you can sell the shares you own freely whenever you want if you find a buyer.
On Seedrs you can invest equity in start-up, invest in a fund (such as the Sustainable Accelerator) or invest in convertible loans that either convert into equity or are going to be paid back with interest.

<table>
<tr><td>Crowdcube (UK)</td><td>1 billion GBP invested</td><td>crowdcube.com</td></tr>
</table>

Crowdcube is fairly like Seedrs (even though they would not want to admit that), however lacks some features such as the mentioned secondary market or the auto invest function. They do however have sustainable investment choices frequently, such as Uniti (electric car company), Polysolar (solar PV windows) or hiyacar (car sharing).

<table>
<tr><td>WeFunder (USA)</td><td>1 billion GBP invested</td><td>wefunder.com</td></tr>
</table>

WeFunder is the US counterpart of the platforms mentioned above. You can invest equity in start-ups that fit your profile, amongst them also sustainable ones such as World Tree (we will talk about them a bit more later).

<table>
<tr><td>Green Rocket (EU)</td><td>NA</td><td>greenrocket.com</td></tr>
</table>

Green Rocket is a bit special in the sense that they specialize in investing in sustainable start-ups. Anything from solar energy to sustainable food is on their website. Having a sustainability focus makes their platform an ideal first start to invest in if you want to get many opportunities to invest capital in companies that fit your focus.

<table>
<tr><td>OnePlanetCrowd (EU)</td><td>NA</td><td>oneplanetcrowd.com</td></tr>
</table>

A Dutch platform where you can invest in sustainable companies, mainly from the Netherlands. They often have innovative companies raising equity, loans, or convertible loans. Some examples are Fairphone (sustainable and modular smartphone) or Snappcar (peer to peer car sharing platform).

Sustainable accelerators
Instead of picking individual start-ups you can invest money in a sustainable accelerator or angel investment fund, often via equity crowdfunding platforms. That way your money gets spread amongst several start-up investment opportunities, but under a clear sustainability angle.

This is like an actively managed fund, with the main difference that the accelerator supports only early-stage companies that fit the investment criteria – in this case sustainability.

They come with very much the same advantages and disadvantages as actively managed funds. One of the main differences is that some of them do not charge fees on the capital you invest, which makes them a highly attractive investment option. They aim to generate most of their return from the exits of some of the start-ups that they invested in. They also focus on early-stage companies and have a clear additionality compared to funds that finance the existing corporations on the stock market.

Investing in an accelerator fund enables you get a diversified portfolio with a one-time investment while the accelerator spreads your capital into several start-ups.

Some examples of accelerators are:
- Sustainable Accelerator https://www.sustainableaccelerator.co.uk/
- Future Planet Capital - https://futureplanetcapital.com

Start-ups with a clear sustainable product or business model
I mentioned a few names above, but which companies could you find on the platforms mentioned above? Here is a brief overview of some:

- Uniti - New mobility concept with an electric car - https://uniti.com/
- Etergo - Sustainable transport with an electric scooter - etergo.com/
- Abundance - Sustainable investment platform - https://www.abundanceinvestment.com/

- Sono Motors - New mobility concept with an electric car - sonomotors.com
- Riversimple - Hydrogen car company - https://www.riversimple.com/
- Fairafric - Fair and in Africa produced chocolate - https://fairafric.com/
- Oddbox - Making food out of rescued vegetables and fruits - https://www.oddbox.co.uk/
- Listnride - Bike rental company - https://www.listnride.com/

Projects with a clear sustainable focus

You can also attain equity in more specific projects if you deem supporting a company is still too broad. This is a bit more of a niche sector which means there are not (yet) as many options available as with the ways of investing equity mentioned above.

You gain even more clarity around where your money goes as you are supporting a very specific use of your funds. This also obviously relates to a higher decision power where you put your money due to that limitation.

However, it is even harder to find these kinds of suitable investment opportunities as it is not common to raise equity from the public for specific projects. That means you also have less opportunities available, leading to a bigger risk if you want to invest a sizable amount of your portfolio in this segment.

One of the examples of such an equity investment (with more details being mentioned later in the reforestation chapter) is World Tree, where you invest in a certain area of trees that are being planted to produce high quality wood. It is not necessarily equity, but also not debt, as it is paid back based on the return on the trees that you own. https://worldtree.info

Commodities

A commodity is a good used in commerce that is relatively interchangeable with other similar goods. Commodities are most often used as inputs in the production of products or services. The quality of any commodity can differ slightly, but it is essentially uniform across producers.

Some examples of commodities include the following:

- Gold
- Oil
- Natural gas

Commodities are an important part of most portfolios as they (depending on the asset) can act as a somewhat store of value through time. Commodities tend to bear a low to negative correlation to traditional asset classes like stocks and bonds. Equities, in particular from the same country, are closely related to each other and tend to have a positive correlation with one another. Commodities, on the other hand, are a bet on unexpected inflation, and they have a low to negative correlation to other asset classes.[15]

There are four ways to invest in commodities:

1. Investing directly in the commodity, either by holding the commodity physically at home or by investing in an exchange-traded fund (ETF) that holds real gold.
2. Using commodity futures contracts to invest.
3. Buying shares of exchange-traded funds (ETFs) that specialize in commodities.
4. Buying shares of stock in companies that produce commodities.

There are many differing opinions around which of the ways of investing in commodities is better. Most individual investors choose ETFs with commodity exposure. Some commodity ETFs buy the physical commodities and then offer shares to investors that represent a certain amount of a particular good.

But to keep things simple and as some ETFs do not keep the actual physical gold in store, I will focus on #1 of investing directly in commodities. There are potential disadvantages to investing directly as you will need to find a buyer and it can be relatively burdensome. But in today's day and age there are several clever ways that you can invest directly in commodities while not having to deal with them physically.

Even though there are many commodities out there, I will focus this chapter on gold as one of the oldest commodities, wood as one of the most sustainable options (even though it has less commodity characterizes than the others) and on Bitcoin as one of the newest ones. Most other commodities such as oil or gas have more of a short-term character, are clearly not sustainable and do not act as a long-term store of wealth.

Gold

Gold has been a store of value for centuries and beyond as it satisfies many criteria for long-term value:

1. **It is and has for centuries been globally accepted as being of value.**
   This makes it easily sell-able across nations and between different cultures and time periods.

2. **Its annual production is not increasing its global stock substantially.**
   Compared to fiat currency that can be printed by central banks, gold needs to be mined. Historically mining has not increased the global gold supply by more than 2-3% of the existing stock, even with jumps in pricing. This makes it very stable in value as increased demand does not lead to a matched increase in supply.

3. **It holds value over time as it cannot be destroyed, nor does it decay.**
   This is crucial as other precious metals can oxidize which therefore does not make them long-term investment opportunities.

Where it falls slightly short is that it cannot be easily traded and be split into small amounts. But with modern technology that is not such a big issue any longer as you can now invest in ETFs that track the gold price or even buy rights to parts of gold bars (so called gold bullions) online.

Having been a standard for investing for centuries, commodities such as gold should be part of any investment portfolio due to enabling a diversified portfolio. It is however not straight-forward when it comes to adding it to a portfolio targeting sustainability at its core.

Environmental Impact

One can argue relatively easily against gold as a sustainable investment. Any form of mining brings with it pollution, thanks to waste material. Given the threat of climate change, mining's use of energy is a more urgent issue, as its large carbon footprint contributes to growing climate instability. All major ways of producing metals, in particular mining, milling, and smelting, are energy intensive.

For precious metals they are even more intense, as large amounts of ore must be processed to produce relatively small amounts of the good – in this case gold.

The sustainability of gold can be questioned due to these processes that are bad for the environment but also often society. These are not directly supported with an investment but are an indirect outcome of the overall gold industry. You are still supporting the demand for gold and as the mining industry is notoriously non-considerate of people or planet it puts it at odds with your investment target of a sustainable return.

One could argue that, because of its high value, the carbon footprint per dollar is not so bad. Calculations by the gold industry itself state that if the gold is held by an investor for somewhere between three and 13 years, its annualized carbon output will be like the overall global economy, therefore not adding extra emissions. This argument has two problems.

Firstly, the impact of the global economy is bad, not good, as the present global economy produces way more carbon dioxide than humanity can live with.

Secondly, any raw material that is held as an investment does nothing actively for society. Your money in gold is not put to productive use compared to investing in companies that try to change our economy. This part of your investment portfolio is rather passive and does not provide value to many people by changing the status quo. Gold's carbon impact is only targeting sustaining status quo, which is clearly the opposite of sustainable.

On the other hand, there are a few ways to look at gold as a neutral investment. Firstly, you do not invest in new production. Most of the gold has been there for a long period as the annual production is around 1-2% of stock levels. It takes time to make a substantial contribution to the existing stock of gold. Due to its high stock to flow ratio, you are not buying new production but rather existing gold already sitting in the bank vaults. And as gold is not destructible, the stock levels are just increasing - while with other raw material annual production often just meets annual demand.

One could argue that there are very little direct emissions associated besides some operational emissions from operating those gold vaults. It must be said though that investing in gold strengthens the gold price and therefore indirectly helps mining companies to exist.

Secondly, holding gold as an investment regarding its usefulness to the economy and a sustainable shift of the economy can be compared to holding cash reserves. Every single person in the Western world holds cash reserves - though the amounts might differ. Surely, those cash reserves are used by banks to do something to the economy, but most of this is negative. Gold might not do anything actively, but at the very least it doesn't continue making a negative impact in the world (if the gold is held privately and not by a bank).

There are new standards being developed such as the Fairmined standard for more sustainable mining, but the production of these niche players is nearly used entirely by the jewelry industry.[16] Close to nothing of it (as of 2023) trickles down into the existing gold reserves.

As you can see, gold is surely more tipping towards the unsustainable side, due to it not having any positive impact. It has however a clear advantage when it comes to inflation, crisis, and climate change impacts - which makes it a portfolio diversification tool.

Social Impact

Gold mining can have a variety of social impacts, both positive and negative.[17]

Economy

Economic impacts can be both positive and negative. As mining can stimulate the local economy and increase the income and opportunities for the population, in many sectors, not just mining. This income is, however, often not shared equally. An unfair distribution of monetary benefits due to bad management or corruption can trigger social tensions. Social conflicts can also arise between companies and illegal miners, as well as anti-mining activists. Increased poverty can also occur if the local population loses traditional means of livelihood, and when governments fail in reinvesting revenues from mining.

Employment and education

The creation of jobs in many sectors, not just the mining sector, is a positive impact of mining activity documented in several studies. If the mining company offers educational opportunities and there is further employee skill development, it can provide additional positive outcomes. Negative impacts here include activities such as child- and forced-labor as well as the quality of jobs. This includes poor and dangerous working conditions, low wages, health impacts, accidents and fatalities, substandard housing provided to workers, lack of freedom in organizing trade unions' activities. For example, increased unemployment can occur due to the mechanization of mining operations.

Social cohesion

The mining activity often attracts workers from other regions causing migration and a change in the local demographic structure. This can lead to a gender imbalance due to the prevalence of male workers, undermining social cohesion and spreading problems of psychological or behavioral nature (e.g., alcoholism, drug addiction, prostitution, rape, etc.). This influx of people can also lead to inflation and rising accommodation costs, which then have a negative effect on the local population.

Social cohesion can be positively affected by creating a bigger market to sell to for the local population.

Environmental
Of course, related to the previous chapter, any effect on the environment will also influence the local population and the human health directly (e.g., having toxic or carcinogenic effects) or indirectly through, e.g., reduced water supply or contamination. Competition for water, an increased water scarcity and depletion are recurrent issues affecting local communities.

General human rights
Violation of human rights can occur in different forms such discrimination of vulnerable groups, lack of inclusion of the local stakeholders and a lack of respect for indigenous populations.

Economic Impact

One of the main arguments for gold to be part of any investment portfolio is its non-correlation with other asset classes. This means that it provides a good portfolio diversification, as it should perform well in an inflation or a recession climate.

Gold must be seen as a long-term investment. There are times where gold will perform poorly (e.g. in period of growth) and therefore one should not be overexposed to gold. It has volatility comparable to stocks in the short-term, which makes it a non-suitable asset if you think short-term. It rather is a store of value that ensures a certain value over longer time horizons.

Gold has a low climate risk. It is not overvalued like fossil fuel companies and not expected to reduce in value during a climate crisis. As in any crisis there is a risk of wealth destruction through regulation or even war, but such a major event would affect most asset classes in an equal manner.

Gold is one of our oldest assets and a relatively liquid asset, depending on the way you invest in the asset itself. With the right services it can be sold faster without major transaction costs.

Rating

Liquidity

New services make investments in gold more liquid than ever before. In the end, the real liquidity of gold heavily depends on how you decide to invest. This rating reflects the option of investing via services such as BullionVault.

Additionality

Investing in gold does not make any meaningful impact and the gold mining industry has been criticized for its practice for a while. As mentioned, there are some exceptions.

Environment

Investing in gold does not have a negative direct impact, but its industry is not having a big positive impact on the environment. With the argument that most gold is already produced; the rating is slightly upgraded by half a star.

Social

Equally, the social impact is at best neutral. However, most gold mining is done in terrible conditions. Since your investment does not directly go to mining, the rating is slightly upgraded by half a star.

Transparency

Gold is a very specific asset, and you know clearly what your capital is invested in.

Effort

Thanks to new platforms it never has been easier and less time consuming to invest in gold.

Risk

Gold is one of the oldest assets and has shown no major loss in value over long-term time horizons. Short-term it can be quite volatile and as any asset it is not 100% risk-free. If you invest via platforms such as BullionVault you also need to consider a third-party risk.

Return

Gold prices can fluctuate with similar volatility as equity. It is hard to project what the returns will be in the future and depending on the time horizon they can even be negative. But over the last 30 returns have been in a 5-12% p.a. range.

Practical Examples

If you deem gold a viable investment alternative and want it as part of your portfolio, what can you do to make it more sustainable?

One way of enabling that change is to support actors in the gold mining industry that truly want to change this status quo. This does not have to be an investment per se, but can be a donation to organizations changing the market, such as Fairmined or the Alliance for Responsible Mining.

Fairmined Gold   https://fairmined.org

Even though there are not many options to buy fairly and ecologically produced investment gold, there are some exceptions. A way of investing instead of supporting through donations is to buy some of the available fairly produced investment gold.

You can buy Fairmined investment gold from some of their suppliers. Note that you will be paying a premium which can influence the possibility to create an economic return on these gold assets.

You can find their partners and suppliers via their official list of suppliers, which can be found at https://drive.google.com/file/d/1xkmUDIo0_zluyKTJOUPBnSp3oaA qkQek/view.

One such example is Fairever Gold. Here you can buy a 1 oz gold bar for a slight extra premium. You can find more details via fairever.gold/gold-bars-coins

---

As there is not much fairly produced gold on the market, you might want to look at changing the industry through other means. As mentioned, most of the gold you are buying has been mined long ago, but the industry still needs to change its practices.

BullionVault   bullionvault.com

BullionVault is mentioned here not because it is another option of sustainable gold, but a convenient option to buy "normal" gold. BullionVault is an investment service where you invest in actual gold that is held in your name at a vault in Zurich, London, Toronto, Singapore, or New York. It is one of the biggest online investment services for gold, managing gold assets worth over 2 billion USD. There is no minimum investment, and the cost of investment is one of the lowest possible due to their economies of scale. Also, you can sell your gold anytime and you can even get the actual gold bars transported to your home (if you have more than 100g).

Fees:
0.50 - 0.05% commission on trading
0.12% commission on total valued stored over a year

Gold backed exchange trade funds (ETFs)

You can also invest in gold backed ETFs, which are securities designed to track the gold price. In those you don't physically own the gold, but rather own a share in the fund owning the metal. Gold ETFs have been around since about 2003. They started in Australia and are now available widely.

You are buying a quoted, gold denominated, debt security which is the obligation of a trust created for the specific purpose of enabling gold investment through it. The trust deed requires the gold denominated debt of the trust to be backed by gold assets which the trust must own - although possibly in various forms. Most of the gold owned by the trust will be in the form of allocated, vaulted Good Delivery Bars.

These ETFs are tradable in most available broker services.

Commission for trading depends on the broker of your choice.
0 - 0.44% p.a.

Name	Ticker	Managed gold (tons)	Fee p.a.
United Kingdom			
iShares Physical Gold ETC	SGLN	227	0.25%
Wisdom Tree Physical Swiss Gold	SGBS	56	0.19%
Wisdom Tree Physical Gold GBP Daily Hedged	GBSP	11	0.39%
Wisdom Tree Physical Gold	PHAU	144	0.39%
Invesco Physical Gold	SGLD	201	0.29%
Gold Bullion Securities Ltd	GBS	83	0.40%
United States			
SPDR Gold Shares	GLD	1,178	0.40%
iShares Gold Trust	IAU	455	0.25%
Sprott Physical Gold Trust	PHYS	72	0.35%
SPDR Gold MiniShares Trust	SPDR	44	0.18%
Aberdeen Standard Physical Gold Shares	SGOL	38	0.17%

Graniteshares Gold Trust	BAR	18	0.18%
Perth Mint Physical Gold ETF	AAAU	6	0.18%
ETFS Physical Precious Metal Basket Shares	GLTR	5	0.60%
VanEck Merk Gold Shares	OUNZ	5	0.40%
Germany/EU			
EUWAX Gold	GOLD	9	0.00%
EUWAX Gold II	EWG2	8	0.00%
Xetra-Gold	4GLD	223	0.36%
Xtrackers Physical Gold ETC	XGLD	23	0.25%
Xtrackers Physical Gold ETC EUR	XAD5	68	0.25%
Xtrackers Physical Gold Euro Hedged ETC	XAD1	59	0.59%
Xtrackers Physical Gold GBP Hedged ETC	XGLS	5	0.69%

Cryptocurrency

Cryptocurrency has been hyped in the last years and there are still new currencies announced on a continuous basis. Most of these will remain a niche, but some have established themselves in the market and can be seen as an investment opportunity - with currently high risks though.

The ones that are most mentioned are Bitcoin and Ether. Bitcoin is the cryptocurrency we will focus on here as it has most commodity-like characteristics and is even seen by the U.S. Securities and Exchange Commission (SEC) as a commodity.

So why on earth would something like Bitcoin be an interesting investment if it is nothing tangible? Well, money itself has no intrinsic value either as its value is purely based on our agreement that it has value. The same applies to Bitcoin - as long as we agree that it has value it is a valid investment. Gold is similar, but it has some intrinsic value as it can be used in processes, but the value of it in those processes is not even close to the value it has as a financial asset.

Over the recent years, financial experts have started recommending cryptocurrencies to be a part of investment portfolios, which is one sign of its value as an investment.

JPMorgan, for example, wrote that "The crypto market continues to mature, and cryptocurrency trading participation by institutional investors is now significant. Bonds may lose their ability to hedge equity portfolios over the next several years, [therefore] less-constrained markets like the yen and gold should form part of long-term hedges, [...] Cryptocurrencies should be added to this list too ... because they can uniquely hedge a yet-unseen environment entailing simultaneous loss of confidence in the domestic currency and its payments system."

Environmental Impact

Bitcoin has a major drawback from an environmental point of view. They need to be "digitally mined" meaning that they require servers that solve complex math problems in order to mine the coins. And as any other process in the "real world" this requires energy. Quite a bit of energy. In the case of Bitcoin, the equivalent energy that is to the whole consumption of all of Ireland.[18]

The problem is all that mining is needed for a cryptocurrency like Bitcoin. It relies on a computational competition called proof of work (PoW). In PoW, all participants race to cryptographically secure transactions and add them to the blockchain's globally distributed ledger. It's a winner-takes-all contest, rewarded with newly minted crypto coins. So, the more computational firepower you have, the better your chances of profit.

PoW mining is difficult by design. The idea is to prevent any one entity from controlling the blockchain. For example, if a bitcoin miner's computer system had more than half of all the mining power on the network, that miner could perpetrate frauds, such as revising long- completed transactions. Bitcoin users would have little recourse because miners are anonymous.

In theory, PoW keeps mining a distributed affair. In practice, however, the development of application-specific ICs (ASICs) that accelerate mining, produced by a handful of chip fabs in China, has concentrated power.

The resultant energy demand has created a backlash from environmentalists. Utilities and communities, meanwhile, see financial risk and opportunity costs if they cater to cryptocurrency miners that gobble up cheap electricity while creating few jobs. Serving miners may require utilities to make equipment upgrades, which could become superfluous if cryptocurrency prices crash and mining operations shut down.

Ethereum moved from PoW to proof of stake (PoS)—an alternative mechanism for distributed consensus. Instead of millions of processors simultaneously processing the same transactions, PoS randomly picks one to do the job. In PoS, the participants are called validators instead of miners, and the key is keeping them honest. PoS does this by requiring each validator to put up a stake—a pile of ether in Ethereum's case—as collateral. A bigger stake earns a validator proportionately more chances at a turn, but it also means that a validator caught cheating has lots to lose.

According to recent research, between 40%[19] to over 50%[20] of the electricity for bitcoin mining comes from renewable sources. This makes bitcoin one of the most renewable large-scale industries in the world. One of the reasons is that Bitcoin miners will use the cheapest sources of energy to make their operations as profitable as possible. In addition, a big portion (still after Chinas crackdown on mining) takes place in China's Sichuan province, which has excessive hydropower capacity. This is good regarding pure CO_2 emissions; however large-scale hydro power in particular has been shown to have huge negative environmental impacts.

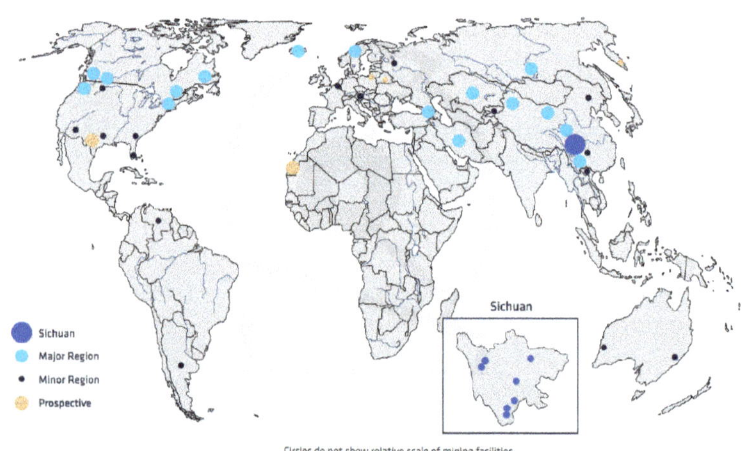

Circles do not show relative scale of mining facilities

Furthermore, over 60% of China's electricity comes from coal. As hydro power is highly seasonal it cannot be a constant energy supply for mining locations, which will lead them to use fossil energies as well. And even if mining uses clean power, it carries the opportunity cost of not using said power for greener purposes, such as charging electric cars, which replace fossil-fuel-guzzling vehicles.

　　　　　　　　　Commodities

One thing to note is that **holding** Bitcoin as a store of value is not directly contributing to emissions caused by mining and trading bitcoins. This only applies if one does only buy bitcoins once and then keeps them stored without trading it for profit in the short-term. In a way it is similar to gold that indirectly the money is invested in an industry that is not actively having a positive impact in the world.

Another emerging concern around bitcoin is electronic waste. The ASIC mining devices required to mine Bitcoin quickly go obsolete, often in just under two years, and they can't really be repurposed for anything other than mining. This is a use of resources that surely has an impact on the climate and needs to be taken into consideration.

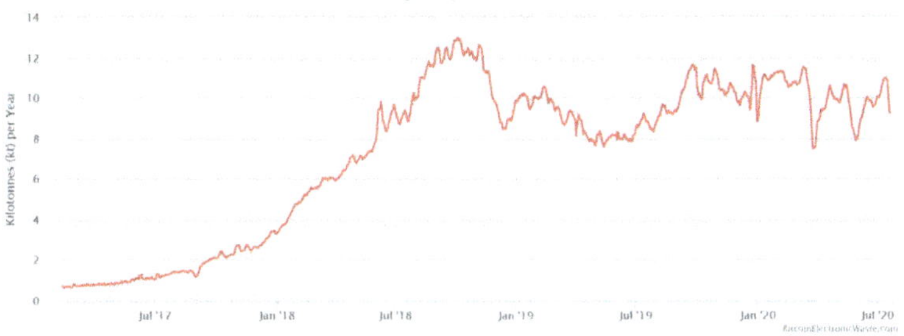

While that is indeed a lot of energy and potential waste, everything we use requires energy and has a waste component. That includes the traditional finance system, from ATMs, credit card transactions or online banking. However, we have far less visibility on the impact these sectors have as the financial system is less transparent than the cryptocurrency industry. One could argue that the cryptocurrency system is built on a more efficient mechanism than our traditional financial sector.

Other sources have also argued that Bitcoin mining can be done anywhere and therefore prefers locations with low costs of electricity. As the cost of renewables is steadily declining and often already lower than fossil fuel alternatives, this should in the long run make miners prefer locations with high shares of renewable energy in the electricity mix. In countries with bad distribution networks mining installations could even act as a local revenue generation for cleaner energy production as the surplus energy from traditional renewable-energy plants could be harnessed to power blockchain computation. This could effectively turn blockchain computing into a renewable subsidy as noted by bitcoin expert Andreas Antonopoulos.[21]

There is also an emerging trend where some mining operations are located near sources of methane emissions. These miners harness the waste methane, which would otherwise be released into the atmosphere, as a low-cost energy source for their operations. This symbiotic relationship between cryptocurrency mining and methane removal not only reduces the environmental impact of both activities but also presents an innovative way to tackle climate change. It showcases the potential for innovative, eco-conscious approaches to energy consumption, benefiting the environment by mitigating greenhouse gas emissions while also powering the digital economy.

In the end it is up to the judgment of each of us if we believe Bitcoin can be part of a sustainable investment strategy. There are arguments for and against it. If you decide in the end to invest in cryptocurrencies, one suggestion would be to restrain from trading it regularly and rather sees it as a storage of value similar to gold.

Social Impact

The social impact of cryptocurrency might not be clear immediately.

Many of us who live in first-world countries take for granted that we can open our smartphones and see that our paycheck was direct deposited, use Apple Pay to buy groceries at the store, or find an ATM in short distance that can give us plenty of cash if needed. But for over 3 billion people on the planet who are unbanked, having access to a workable medium of exchange is to this day a huge challenge.

One example is Venezuela. Venezuela has been the perfect symbol for a currency crisis for decades. According to a report in Reuters[22], annual inflation in Venezuela in May 2018 was over 24,600% for the previous 12-month period. Excessive money printing and shortages of crucial food items and medicine compound the problems and caused the Venezuelan bolivar to lose 98% of its value during 2018.

Of course, Venezuelans do not trust their government-run banks after having had to endure inflation for decades. Cryptocurrencies are finally giving many people around the world, not only Venezuelans, a democratic and stable option for digital currencies not under centralized control.

In other parts of the world people move to developed countries to work, but still send home remittances to support their family. They often use services such as Western Union to do so. It is a platform which helps people send and receive money all over the world. However, between their own fees, wire transfer fees, conversion fees and other hidden fees, you can lose close to 16% of your entire transferred amount. For people that often are already on surviving on the minimum income, this is an unbearable burden. With cryptocurrencies such as Bitcoin you can transfer money anywhere for low cost, enabling the families to receive more value to spend on their necessities. In many countries exchanging Bitcoin for cash is still difficult though and would need to be solved by either having access to Bitcoin ATMs or by being able to pay in Bitcoin.

Most importantly, for many people that are under- or unbanked, being able to put their money into a different asset than cash can be the only investment option besides planting crops or buying cattle. Often rural communities keep their savings in cash at home, which poses not only a risk of being robbed but also makes them vulnerable to impacts on the currency and does not let them earn interest on their hard-earned savings. By putting some of their money into cryptocurrency they can not only remove the risk of being robbed, but also increase their financial wealth by taking advantage from the potential value increase and inflation hedge.

On the negative side many have argued that bad actors such as terrorist groups benefit from the use of Bitcoin as it enables them to finance their operations while staying anonymous. However, there have been several cases by now where law enforcement could identify terrorist groups and their transactions through their Bitcoin wallets and seize their assets. In such cases, using cryptocurrency becomes a disadvantage as all transactions are publicly accessible and can be traced back to the origin. By and large, the majority of terrorism is still financed through Fiat currency and will likely remain that way.[23]

Outside of Bitcoin and Ethereum there are also other projects that utilize the blockchain for a social impact, but for the sake of this book we will focus on only these two.

Economic Impact

It is relatively easy to liquidate your bitcoins as everything is done online in exchanges. There are still some friction elements behind it but as long as you liquidate bitcoins below the daily limits of exchanges it is a liquid asset. In addition, Bitcoin can be split into smaller values than any other currency and most precious metals - in a simple way at the very least. This makes it easily scalable to any size and enables it to increase in value without impeding smaller transactions through it.

Bitcoins can also be sent from anywhere in the world to anywhere else in the world. No bank can block payments or close your account. Bitcoin is censorship resistant money. It enables cross border payments, and also provides an easy way for people to escape failed government monetary policy.

Billions of people around the world lack access to banking infrastructure and traditional means of finance like credit. With Bitcoin, these individuals can send value across the globe for close to no fee. Bitcoin's true potential as a means of banking for those without access to traditional banks has perhaps yet to be fully developed.

Bitcoin also provides sound and predictable monetary policy that can be verified by anyone. It is difficult to corrupt, thanks to its encrypted, decentralized system and complicated algorithms. It doesn't rely on a central verifier but has everyone verify the transaction (ledger). This makes it nearly impossible to attack it and alter its transactions. As such, Bitcoin is one of the safest investment assets imaginable, as long as the investor uses it correctly. Giving the digital keys to the wrong person can still lead to a full loss of one's assets.

One of the reasons gold is an investment asset is because there is a limited amount of gold on earth. There is always less and less gold left to be mined and it becomes harder and more expensive to find and mine. Because of that and with Gold's long history as a medium of exchange, it is considered a hedge against inflation. The same applies to Bitcoin. There will only be 21 million Bitcoins, and over time, it will be harder and harder to mine remaining ones left. With those assumptions, many argue that Bitcoin will reach the global valuation of gold in the medium-term.

Bitcoin, Ethereum and cryptocurrency more generally are new phenomenon and being so carries a big risk for early adopters. Important for widespread adoption is also usability. Currently, cryptocurrencies are still inherently complicated to use and require time to get used to. This can be seen as a major obstacle, in particular for investors that are not willing to spend longer periods of time getting to understand how cryptocurrencies such as Bitcoin can be used.

As its predicted value increase is hinging on it becoming globally accepted and even replacing - or at least joining - gold as a store of value, it has many hurdles to overcome. These might prove in the end too big for its mass adoption and could lead to a loss of or complete wipe-out of their value. There is also a possibility of an improvement to the Bitcoin model through a new cryptocurrency that could make Bitcoin obsolete.

Another major concern for investors looking toward Bitcoin as a safe haven asset is its volatility. One needs to look only to the price history of Bitcoin in the last two years for evidence. At its highest point, around the beginning of 2018, Bitcoin reached a price of about $20,000 per coin. About a year later, the price of one Bitcoin hovered around $4,000. Over the long term it is predicted that this volatility will decrease, but it is close to impossible to predict when exactly that will happen.

Commodities

Rating

Liquidity

Due to their digital nature cryptocurrencies are one of the most liquid assets in the market.

Additionality

While the impact is not as positive, the additionality with Bitcoin is that it is a relatively new asset class.

Environment

There is an argument that the environmental impact is not as bad as many think. But to be conservative the rating for Bitcoin is somewhere between negative and neutral.

Social

Due to factors mentioned later, the social impact however can be substantial.

Transparency

Most cryptocurrency, and Bitcoin in particular, are very transparent assets.

Effort

It is becoming simpler to invest in this asset, but there is still a learning curve that prohibits them from widespread use.

Risk

Cryptocurrency is the newest asset class in our economy and has and will continue to be highly volatile.

Return

Cryptocurrency and Bitcoin have historically shown tremendous returns. If Bitcoin succeeds, the returns can be tremendous. But there is a huge risk that this will not be met.

Practical Examples

Be aware that the mentioned tips below apply to most other cryptocurrencies as well, not only Bitcoin (even though there might be slight differences depending on the actual currency).

For a long time, cryptocurrencies have been one of the most difficult assets to invest in as you needed to set up relatively complicated wallets.

That is partly still the case, in particular if you want to be 100 percent sure about the safety of your investment. However, there are increasingly more services that make it easier to buy Bitcoin. These save your cryptocurrency in their cloud service though and are vulnerable to hacking attacks as has been seen with the Mt. Gox example.[24]

Buying on exchanges

To get started you need to buy bitcoins from an exchange or other places. The advantage of buying them from an exchange is that you can send them later to other services (more below), while many non-exchange service providers limit your ability to send the bitcoins outside of your account with them.

Some exchanges are listed below. This is by no means an exhaustive list, but some of the simpler exchanges out there are:

- Kraken – kraken.com
- Binance – binance.com
- Coinbase – coinbase.com

On all of these sites you need to create an account first and go through the verification process before you can buy cryptocurrency. This should not take more than a few days in general. After you are verified, you can send FIAT currency to your account with the exchange and buy the wanted cryptocurrency. The suggestion is to not leave your bitcoins in the exchange but transfer it to another place, such as a physical ledger.

Physical ledger

One option is still to transfer your bitcoins to a physical ledger that you can store at home. It is safe in the sense that it is not stored online, that way nobody can steal your bitcoins through hacking any online wallet. but the risk of losing such a wallet is also higher than having it online.

They work by generating a user's private keys in a secure, offline environment and have an easy-to-use display. You can connect them via USB or Bluetooth to internet-connected devices like your computer. A separate screen on the wallet is used to verify and approve transactions, helping to prevent the sharing of sensitive information to the internet-connected device. This all combines to be very handy as you don't have to worry about a computer being compromised.

NGRAVE

Dubbed the "coldest wallet" in the industry, the device doesn't allow you to connect to the internet in any way. Rather than using a USB port or Bluetooth, the ZERO uses one-way QR code communication to relay information to connected devices while staying offline. All of this means that you will never have to worry about compromised software.

Ledger Nano X

The Ledger Nano X, from a France-based start-up company, looks like a typical USB thumb drive except with a steel shell. The device can be connected to any mobile devices or a personal computer with a USB or Bluetooth. The device supports over 30 cryptocurrencies including Bitcoin, Ethereum, Dash, Litecoin, Tron, and more. This is the most popular hardware wallet to date — aided in part by Ledger's huge marketing effort over the years.

Keepkey

The KeepKey is similarly shaped to the Ledger, however, it features an easy-to-read digital display. Its parent company, Shapeshift, is a long time and trusted software wallet provider in the crypto space.

Buying bitcoins on other services

There are services that have cryptocurrency as an asset that can be purchased through them even though the main purpose of the service provider might be something else. One of the major caveats with such services is often that you cannot send your coins to other platforms but have to buy and sell on the same platform provider.

Revolut

One such example is Revolut. Revolut, being one of the forefront digital banks in Europe, has started to offer buying cryptocurrency inside your Revolut account. It is relatively straightforward and easy to buy, but you can (as of now) not send all of the cryptocurrencies outside of the Revolut account. Bitcoin and Ethereum work, however.

PayPal

Another one is PayPal, on which you can buy a few crypto currencies, including Bitcoin. It also allows you to send the crypto to your own wallet afterwards.

Reforestation

By investing in this investment asset, you provide the finance needed to buy land, plant, and maintain a certain amount of trees. Depending on the business model these trees are then sporadically deforested to produce wood or the trees themselves produce food that is then sold, such as olives or chocolate beans. This should all be done under a sustainable farming and harvesting approach.

Owning forests could be seen as a form of real estate as land prices generally increase as do apartments or houses. But at the same time forests produce wood, which can be seen as a commodity - even though there are some differences between different wood types. Then again, sometimes you have a more or less defined repayment schedule with your forest investment, with a somewhat defined return (although depending on the wood price), which puts this investment into the bond category. And lastly, owning forests/land can be seen as equity as you own part of an asset as you do when you hold shares in a company.

For the sake of simplicity, I put reforestation into the commodity asset as the main cash flow from forests often comes from commodities such as wood or produce.

Investing in forests has been proven as an investment class by big corporations that utilize monocultures and heavy machinery. However, the ways one can invest today with more sustainable practices and new companies have not been proven on a bigger scale. This can increase the risk of this asset type and put it in a similar bucket as start-up investing. A lot of the risk here lies in the companies offering these investment opportunities and how successful their business model is.

Environmental impact

This is one of the most active and promising approaches to reduce our emissions and CO_2 concentration in the atmosphere. With an investment in reforestation, you can be close to certain that your money is off-setting greenhouse gas emissions. It is one of the few investment opportunities that can have a positive effect on local ecosystems and biodiversity if done right. Some or most of the trees planted will be cut after 10-20 years, but if such a system is well managed, it shouldn't be an issue to cut trees.

Investing in wood production can also lead to ripple effects in our economies. For example, by supporting reforestation, the increase of trees and with it the availability of wood, products that have been produced in plastic might go back to wood. That can include things such as guitars and surf boards among others as World Tree has shown so far. Doing so would lead to a lower burden on the environment in general.

According to a research paper in Science[25], planting billions of trees globally could be one of the biggest and most resourceful ways of remove CO_2 out of the atmosphere (without encroaching on crop land or urban areas). They could absorb up to 57bn tons of CO_2 in this century according to the IPCC[26]. As is known, trees absorb and store carbon dioxide while they grow. If we would engage in a global planting program, we could remove 2/3 of the human caused emissions in the atmosphere today. Scientists identified over 1.7bn hectares of treeless land that could host over 1.2tn native trees. That is about 11% of all land masses or the similar to the US and China combined. Scientists excluded all land that is currently used to grow crops and urban areas from this analysis. They did include grazing land as there are a few trees that could also benefit the grazing animals. This has a tremendous potential and is simultaneously mind-blowing and obvious.

However, to achieve this of course it is assumed that (if the trees are cut) the wood is not being burned but used in ways in which it doesn't release its CO_2 in a short period of time. Therefore, you need to be diligent in picking your reforestation service that you want to invest in and often even then it is hard to have a full judgment. Forests that are being used as biofuel sources later on will not significantly reduce the CO_2 concentration in the atmosphere over the long-term - even though they still contribute at a time that it is crucial to start reducing our emissions as a civilization.

Even though trees and forests are generally beneficial, there is a risk that you choose to invest in mono-culture forests. These might off-

Commodities

set a good amount of CO_2, but do not contribute to the ecosystem. You need to ensure to the level you need to feel comfortable that the companies or projects you invest in have a more holistic view. Agroforestry projects could be one such aspect of forests that are planting a more diverse set of trees.

An assessment published in the journal Nature shined light on that fact. Forest researchers looked at the small print of government declarations about what type of forests they are creating. They found that around 45 percent of those new forests will be monoculture plantations of fast-growing trees like acacia and eucalyptus, usually planted to make pulp for paper. Such forests often decrease biodiversity rather than increase it and can often only hold a small fraction of the carbon that could be captured by natural forests. Another 21 percent of the reforestation would plant fruit and other trees on farms as part of agroforestry programs. Which leaves us with just 34 percent that are planned to be natural forests.

But as you are not investing in government programs this only partially applies to the investments taken by yourself. But it shows how important it is to pick the right investment in this category. It is one of the most impactful and most proactive impact investment assets you can add to your portfolio if your choice is made right.

Social Impact

This investment segment creates jobs in emerging markets where the other main opportunity for income often is agricultural, which involves cutting down forests to create farmland. As many companies offering sustainable forestry are conscious about the overall impact of their work, they tend to go even a step further in that they not only create jobs but also try to provide fair working conditions for their employees.

In the example of Forest Finance, they have principles in place of being a fair workplace. This ranges from gender equality, employing local indigenous people to providing education to their employees. Even more so they offer health care and micro-loans to their employees and actively prevent any form of child labor.

Done right, (re-)forestation projects have a big potential in making a difference for the local population. They can lead to significant increases in life quality for people doing these jobs through education, an income and proper work practices.

Economic Impact

Returns to investors in forestry are made up of sales of timber, sales of other goods and services, increases in the value of the woodland (from annual increment or market factors), and the net income from subsidies (e.g., planting grants) less taxes. For example, estimates of the return from forestry are produced annually in the Investment Property Databank (IPD) UK Forestry Index, available at www.msci.com/www/ipd-factsheets/ipd-uk-annual-forestry-index/0163322597. The index shows a total return of 11.6% per annum for the three-year period 2015 to 2017, and an annual return of 13.9% for 2017.

Investments in forests are less correlated to the global markets. Whatever happens in the wider economy, your wealth is still growing because your trees are growing. This makes trees a great inflation-proof store of wealth and means that even if the economy is in a downward cycle and other investments are performing poorly, forestry should still be earning your returns.

It's also a flexible investment in terms of inventory – if the market price is too low for one year, it is possible to leave the trees standing. Not only is there close to no cost besides minor operational costs, but the amount of timber harvested the following year will have increased. Having investments in more commonly held assets such as wood reduces risk and is one of the key benefits of alternative investments.

Investments in forestation generally have a long tenor and there is often close to no possibility of selling your investment early on a secondary market. You need to ensure that you invest capital that you will not need in the next 10 to 20 years. This is one of the reasons that this asset class should not be a huge part of your portfolio, in particular if you rely on that money being available short-term.

Many of the companies that are suggested here do not have a track record when it comes to repayments to investors. Therefore, it is difficult to judge their investment case currently. As these investment opportunities are on separate platforms, they increase the complexity of your portfolio. But you will not need to worry about re-balancing as your money is locked in for a long period of time.

Rating

Liquidity

This investment has a poor liquidity as trees first need to grow before there is any value in the land invested in.

Additionality

Investing in reforestation projects that aim to bring with them diversity and keeping parts of the forest after harvest is the most impactful asset you can invest in.

Environment

This is an investment asset that really shines in this category. As you are investing in trees that off-set carbon this is a net-positive investment, assuming you pick a non-monoculture investment such as some mentioned later.

Social

The social impact of your investment here is slightly less clear, but assuming you invest in an ethical reforestation company it is also one of the highest.

Transparency

Most of the time it is clear what your money will be used for as you are buying either land with future forest or a certain number of trees.

Effort

You will have to do more manual work in the investment process than with stocks, but due there not being much liquidity in your invested capital you do not have to worry about re-balancing and reinvesting your capital.

Risk

On the positive side you are investing in an asset that has shown value increase over long periods of time. However, most of the investment companies offering this to investors with small ticket sizes are early-stage and have not shown a proof of return to most of their investor base yet.

Return

Most reforestation investment assets are able to return 5-7% p.a. There are exceptions with returns in the 7-10% p.a. range, but they are often not as environmentally friendly.

Practical Examples

World Tree	**Minimum 1,000-2,000 USD**	https://worldtree.eco

World Tree is a US based organization that plants Empress trees in the US and parts of Latin America. The Empress Splendor tree is one of the fastest growing trees in the world, reaching maturity within 10 years. It is a non-invasive, hybrid species, that can grow in many parts of the United States and Canada, where its primary use is lumber. Empress Splendor trees are not genetically modified but are bred by conventional methods used by farmers for thousands of years. They do not respond well to chemical products, preferring organic farming methods and the use of natural fertilizers such as chicken manure. When you cut down an Empress tree it regrows from the stump. An Empress tree will regenerate like this up to 7 times, continuing to absorb carbon for over 50 years.

With World Tree, you invest in an area in which Empress trees will be planted. The money raised each year funds that year's planting of trees, or 'vintage'. The saplings are distributed from World Tree partner nurseries in Canada, USA, Guatemala, Mexico, and Costa Rica to the farmers enrolled in the program.

The farmers provide the land and work to grow the trees and World Tree provides the trees and its management expertise. If those trees are successfully harvested, investors can receive distributions after 8-12 years: 50% of the profit goes to the farmers directly and 25% each to World Tree and the investor.

For an investment of around 4,000 USD, you can expect a return of around 13,000 USD, which is with 13% p.a. a lucrative investment.

It has to be noted that nobody has received their investment back from WeFunder due to the long-time windows and the young age of the company. In addition, as World Tree is focusing on the Empress trees, there is the risk of monoculture and negative effects on the environment.

Forest Finance	Minimum 400 EUR	https://www.forestfinance.de/en/

Forest Finance is a Germany based organization that plants and manages sustainable forest in Latin America and North Africa. They have several different investment products depending on what you want to invest in:

Oasis

Here you invest in organic agroforestry with dates and olives. The investment term is relatively short with only 6 years. During this period, you benefit from the profits of selling olives and dates and in year 6 of the proceeds from the sale of the trees. The return is expected to be around 5% p.a.

Forest Savings Plan

Here you invest in an ecological mixed forest in Panama and receive the proceeds from the sale of wood after harvesting. After about 13 and 19 years you receive the first returns from the first thinning of trees, which is a selective cutting of trees throughout the forest. In year 25 more trees are harvested and you earn a return from the sale of these bigger pieces of wood. Forest Finance claims to not harvest all trees of the planted forest as it is aiming to maintain the remaining forest afterwards. You can expect a return of 4-5% p.a. over 25 years.

The advantage with Forest Finance is that they plant mixed forests with more impact on the local economy, environment and society than just producing wood. They also aim to maintain forests that have been partially cleared once. Based on these goals the risk of investing in a monoculture or bad practices seem rather low.

Sharewood   https://www.sharewood.com/en

Sharewood is similar to Forest Finance in the sense that they plant trees in Latin America. During a period of 20 years, they select-cut portions of the forest and sell the wood on the market to then pay you out a partial repayment. They offer similar interest rates of 6 to 11% p.a. However, they do so by focusing on monocultures that at the end of the 20-year planting cycle get clear-cut.

The lists above are an overview of places you can invest in trees. They cover mainly investment offers that are accessible to people with the smallest pocket (e.g., low investment sizes) and companies that seem to do the right thing. There are other investment opportunities out there, but often they support only monocultures or have minimum investment sizes that are not affordable by the average investor.

Real Estate

Investing in real estate can take many shapes, from owning and renting out an apartment/house to investing via alternative platforms. It is a rather traditional investment asset and has been the main way of becoming rich for many.

As there are so many alternatives to investing in real estate, the sustainability of those investments can have a wide range. It can go from sustainable investments such as net-positive energy houses, social housing, or renovation projects to negative impact ones such as the "development" of a forest area to a shopping mall or residential area.

Environmental impact

Actually, many construction materials have a big climate impact, such as concrete, so in order to be environmentally sustainable one needs to be very good in the due diligence to pick only climate positive projects to invest in. There are different layers of environmental impact, from the worst of turning fertile land into real estate to rebuilding or renovating existing houses with sustainable materials.

It is definitely not the first place you should look at when investing your money sustainably, as the real estate sector has a serious impact on climate change. Buildings account for nearly 40% of energy related CO2 emissions and consume 35% of the world's energy.[27]

Your money is also not put to productive use compared to investing in companies or projects directly. There can be exceptions, such as investing in green housing, but generally real estate does not contribute to a positive change when it comes to climate change. Therefore, you most often see real estate as a passive part of your portfolio that does not offset any emissions or worse a part of your portfolio whose climate impact you have to compensate for.

However, there is potential with sustainable real estate. Green-certified buildings generally have positive sale and higher rental premiums, as well as operating costs up to 14% lower and 9% higher occupancy rates compared to non-green buildings.[28]

One needs to be very diligent when deciding to invest in a real estate object. Some ways of doing so are:

1. Invest in real estate utilizing alternative building materials that replace existing ones, in particular concrete. That can be anything from wood to clay and other natural materials such as rammed earth.
2. Focus on renovation over completely new developments due to its much smaller carbon footprint.
3. Focus on real estate that aims at incorporating better ways of resource usage, such as rainwater collection, green roofs, and sustainable energy such as solar panels and energy independence of the building.
4. Renting out part of your own home will reduce the need to build another house for someone else, e.g., with a townhouse. This can even generate passive income that can off-set your loan repayments for the townhouse itself.

Finding investment opportunities in green certified buildings, however, requires a lot more work as there are less options out there at the moment. Therefore, you might want to keep your portfolio's share of real estate relatively low - if you don't plan to invest in your own house as you of course need a place to live.

Social Impact

Since social impact through real estate can only be generated in the way the property is operated and not just by owning the property, investors in property have to ensure the 'impact-driven' operation of their developments - either by investing in or setting up an operating company, or by choosing a capable partner.

Social impact in real estate can take many shapes. Providing affordable housing for low-income parts of the population or individuals with disabilities is one. Affordable housing and support can generate valuable social impact, as it meets a basic need for shelter and can help to achieve other positive social benefits such as better health, stronger communities, improved employment opportunities and reduced crime.[29]

Another key area for social impact for real estate investments is the ageing part of our populations, in particular in developed nations in e.g., Europe. A dynamically growing elderly population, a higher demand for different types of care provision and additional services promoting health and wellbeing of the elderly are the main drivers in this segment. Opportunities could arise in niche sectors, such as high-quality care homes or innovative residential care/assisted living concepts with a real estate component, which may overlap with supported affordable housing for the elderly.

Finding clear social impact opportunities in the real-estate sector, in particular as a retail investor, can prove to be quite challenging. And if you want to combine them with environmental impact simultaneously, it becomes even more niche.

The simplest way to be sure about social impact is to focus your search on investment opportunities in elderly care or affordable housing.

Economic Impact

Real estate is a non-cash, so called "hard" investment and an asset that is a hedge against inflation. It maintains or even increases in value during a period where the non-tangible investment world, in particular cash for example, loses value. This makes it an excellent asset to diversify your portfolio with.

It also can provide you with a passive income when done right. If you own a good piece of real estate that can be rented out easily at high value, you could earn a passive income and a return on investment after a certain period. By doing so you could instead of paying rent for the place you live in get rental payments from subtenants that in turn pay your mortgage and in the long run provide you with an "interest free" home.

Real estate can also be seen as less volatile as long as there is no mortgage bubble. This can make it a relatively stable investment, in particular in places where there is a lot of demand for housing.

However, in bigger crises the returns in real estate can be affected by fluctuations in other markets, such as the stock market. The rise and fall of major stock indexes can trigger a variety of reactions and behaviors that can indirectly affect the way people choose to buy and sell their homes. Although there is no direct link between these two markets, it is possible that significant action in either can influence the behavior of the other. Which in turn has an effect on the stability of this asset.

Real estate is also not the most liquid asset, meaning it often cannot be sold quickly. There are higher transaction costs than in most other assets and selling it requires more work than selling shares, for example. If you need your cash quickly, it can mean that you will have to sell your real estate below market value. Therefore, you should consider carefully how much money you want to put into real estate.

Diversification is also difficult as you often need substantial amounts of capital to invest in the real estate market. There are alternatives which we will cover later that allow you to buy small shares of real estate projects. But if you want to own a house or several apartments, you will need to invest amounts that might prove to be a majority or even all of your available investment capital. This makes it harder to diversify overall both from an asset as well as a geographic exposure.

Rating

Liquidity

Most real estate investment options discussed in this chapter are relatively liquid with paybacks in 3+ years. If you buy your own real estate to also live in its liquidity would be lower.

Additionality

Additionality is quite high assuming you finance the renovation or construction of new infrastructure. The rating would be lower if you just buy shares in an existing apartment.

Environment

Renovation projects or net-positive energy houses will be better than investing in "developing" forest properties. The rating is assuming a focus on impactful real estate.

Social

The use case of the finalized real estate project is more important for the social impact. Investments in elderly homes or housing for homeless people will score higher while most commercial buildings will be low. The rating is assuming a focus on impactful real estate.

Transparency

With most real estate investments, you know exactly what your money is being used for.

Effort

Investments in real estate platforms as discussed later are less time intensive than investing in a real estate object yourself. You still have to actively pick your investment and manage it though.

Risk

Development projects are generally higher risk than buying existing real estate with tenants and rental payments.

Return

This depends to some extent if you finance the construction of real estate with a loan or if you buy portions of existing real estate assets. But generally, real estate has been performing well. For the rating we assume a construction/renovation loan.

Practical Examples

As mentioned, there are many ways to invest in real estate, the ones below are just to highlight some of them.

Buying your own place

The most straight forward way is to buy your own real estate that you live in. Best case you buy a house that can be compartmentalized and partially rented out to a tenant. By doing so you generate income that you can use to pay off the mortgage or reinvest it. You can also aim at buying a property in bad shape and renovate it, therefore removing the need to build one new house in the market. This can also include energy efficiency investments in your house, such as better insulation, solar energy on the roof to off-set energy usage, sustainable heating such as geothermal or solar thermal and so on.

Alternative investment possibilities

If you don't have the means to buy a real estate asset or don't want to take such a big debt burden on yourself, you can invest in real estate via alternative platforms. In many countries nowadays you can invest via so called "crowdfunding" or "crowdinvesting platforms".

The big advantage of investing via crowdfunding is that you can spread your risks in this asset class into several baskets. You can invest in several countries in different currencies, sometimes even on different continents. If you have limited funds, you can avoid having to put all your money in one real estate object (if it is not the one you are living in).

     Real Estate

Debt financing

Here you really finance the construction or renovation of real estate by providing the debt needed. You receive an interest rate and after several years are paid back interest and amortization.

Advantages	
High return	You are getting an above market return on your capital, as most interest rates are above 10% p.a. This makes it highly interesting as an investment opportunity.
Diversification	You can diversify your capital into several investments, which means that you are hedging your bets and reducing your risks
Disadvantages	
Liquidity	Even though the tenor of loans being financed is only between 1 to 3 years, your capital is locked in that period and in most cases, you cannot sell your stake during the period. That means that your investment is very illiquid and if you need capital in the short-term you will need to sell other assets.
Risk	In case you finance a new construction, you are taking the upfront risk of construction, while not receiving most of the upside of that risk as you often don't own equity. This can be reduced by taking a charge over the asset.
Environmental Impact	Debt financing in most cases has a bigger environmental impact as you often finance new construction buildings. An exception would be renovation, but those investment opportunities are relatively rare compared to new developments.

Equity financing
Through equity financing you actually own a part of a real estate building or apartment. You can sell your part later on for a higher price and earn a passive income through the rent generated by the real estate you own.

Advantages	
Value Increase	You own equity of a real estate asset, which gives you the upside in the case that the value increases. This makes sense in investments where you would take the construction risk.
Passive Income	You can earn a passive income through the rent payments. And as you can diversify your portfolio a lot more than owning your own house, you are not relying on only one tenant being on time with their payments.
Diversification	You can diversify your capital in different rental properties. This helps you with a potential return on your equity when you want to sell your stake in the building. As you can have assets in different geographies and currencies, you are less likely to face a housing bubble in all your real estate investments at the same time.
Disadvantages	
Work	It takes a lot of work to diversify thoroughly in your assets. You will have to use different platforms in different currencies, setup accounts on all these platforms and track your investments in different locations.

Time Horizon	If you want to take advantage of the equity nature of your investment, you will need to keep your capital invested for an even longer time than with debt. You can sell whenever you want, meaning your investment is highly liquid, but you should hold on to your asset for at least 5 years if you want to make a meaningful return on the equity increase.
Environmental Impact	Debt financing in most cases has a bigger environmental impact as you are often financing the new construction of buildings. The only exception here would-be renovation, but those investment opportunities are relatively rare compared to new developments.

Below you can find several examples for both debt and equity platforms in the real estate space. This list is of course not exclusive but should give you an idea where you can start investing if the alternative real estate investment space is for you.

Tessin, EU/Sweden	**Minimum 10,000 – 50,000 SEK**	https://tessin.com/en

Tessin is a Swedish real estate crowdfunding platform where you can invest in Swedish real estate projects. They offer real estate debt which is mostly targeting new developments. Regarding where to invest the same guidelines from above apply, so if you follow those you can ensure a more climate friendly investment.

Crowdestate, EU   **Minimum 100 EUR**   https://crowdestate.eu

Crowdestate is lending based platform which allows you to invest in two categories of real estate loans: rental and development. While the rental category finances projects with cash flow from rents, the development category finances projects in constructing and selling buildings. Few opportunities are also available for business investment under corporate finance that provides funding for sea-food shops, factories, and construction companies. The platform provides investment across Latvia, Estonia, and Italy. An investor is required to lend money to get

monthly interests with the invested money being paid back periodically.

In order to keep your investments here as green as possible you want to focus on renovation projects or anything similar. You want to avoid land development or completely new constructions as these are having a bad effect on the climate.

Bulkestate, EU   **Minimum 50 EUR**   https://www.bulkestate.com

On Bulkestate you can either lend to real estate developers or buy shares in real estate assets such as apartments. In that way you would actually own a real estate asset, but without the hassle of setting up everything yourself, while getting a good discount.

Similarly, if you decide to lend to developers you want to ensure that it does not include land development and new constructions, but rather renovations. If you buy shares in existing real estate such as apartments, then the story is slightly different as those do not have too much of an active footprint. However, you might want to avoid non-energy efficient apartments.

<table>
<tr><td>EstateGuru, EU</td><td>Minimum 50 EUR</td><td>https://estateguru.co</td></tr>
</table>

Similar to Tessin, EstateGuru lets you invest in real estate projects via loans. These loans are potentially lower risk, but you still carry a currency risk / inflation risk in your investments. Regarding where to invest the same guidelines from above apply, so if you follow those you can ensure a more climate friendly investment.

<table>
<tr><td>London House Exchange, UK</td><td>Minimum 50 GBP</td><td>londonhouseexchange.com</td></tr>
</table>

In London House Exchange you own a share in a real estate asset and receive your share of the profit from the rents paid by tenants. Here the minimum size is much lower, which enables you to build a well-diversified portfolio of real estate assets. This way of investing is probably the most environmentally friendly option in this list as you are buying existing real estate assets from existing investors.

The goal is to find investment opportunities on these sites that match your investment focus and values. That means you should keep an eye out as these opportunities do not appear regularly.

A tangible example for a sustainable real-estate investment through these platforms is a renovation project on CrowdEstate in Milan. In it the developer aims to do a complete renovation and energy re-qualification of a building that is currently in a state of neglect (the current status of it can be seen below).

Figure 4 - Captures from CrowdEstate

Renovation works will include:
- Improving the energy efficiency of the whole building.
- Refurbishment of the external facades with the installation of a thermal coat.
- Installation of new fixtures.
- Installation of photovoltaic panels, heat pumps and air conditioning.
- Installation of a new elevator.

Figure 5 - Capture from CrowdEstate

Although not perfect (hardly any investment is unfortunately), this one shows a clear aim to be more environmentally friendly by using existing infrastructure, making it more energy efficient and adding renewable energy production to it. The social impact of the project is less clear, but in this example the selling price of the apartments is slightly below the market price which makes it a bit more affordable if only by a small margin.

Bonds

Bonds are commonly referred to as fixed income securities. They are a form of debt as you are lending money to an entity such as a government, corporation or bank who is issuing the bond (issuer). The issuer is generally obliged to pay interest at set intervals (coupons) over the bond's life (term) and then repay the principal amount (nominal or face value) when the bond matures.

Bonds can be in mutual funds or can be in private investment where a person would give a loan to a company or the government.

A bond is a form of loan or IOU: the holder of the bond is the lender (creditor), the issuer of the bond is the borrower (debtor), and the coupon is the interest. There are bonds that are ear-marked to certain use cases, such as green bonds for sustainable projects. And other bonds that are more a general lending of a company or state for its everyday operations.

Most bonds can be sold by the initial lender to other investors after the bond has been issued. In other words, a lender does not have to hold a bond until the end of its maturity date. It can also happen that bonds are repurchased by the borrower if interest rates decline, or if the borrower's credit has improved, and it can reissue new bonds at a lower cost.

There are several types of bonds and the ones we will cover in the following chapters are:

Government Bonds

Government bonds such as those issued by governments. There are sub-categories of government bonds depending on their maturity, but the entire category of bonds issued by a government treasury is often collectively referred to as "treasuries."

Municipal Bonds
Municipal bonds are issued by states and municipalities. We do not go into specific detail on those but have some examples under government bonds.

Corporate Bonds
These are bonds issued by companies. Companies issue bonds rather than seek bank loans for debt financing in many cases because bond markets offer more favorable terms and lower interest rates.

All the above can be categorized based on their maturity.

Long-term Bonds
Long-term bonds are affected by the prevailing interest rate environment and are therefore not a great hedge against economic recessions.

Short-term Bonds
Short-term bonds are less affected by economic recessions and can therefore be good hedges for such scenarios. The permanent portfolio treats these as a form of cash.

Government Bonds

Governments have always been the largest issuers of debt. When an investor is buying government bonds, they are lending money to the government for a certain number of years. In return, they receive interest payments at regular intervals on the loan they have given, while the face-value of the bond remains unchanged, and the amortization is paid off in a lump-sum at the end of the term.

For everyday investors these bonds are close to impossible to buy sometimes. However, there are funds that focus on bonds which then in turn enable other investors to get exposure to these investments' assets.

Environmental and Social Impact

It is hard to assess the impact of your investment. Investing in government bonds is likely one of the least transparent assets mentioned in this book. As you are most often investing in a government in general, you support their activities more broadly, which includes construction of infrastructure. There are some exceptions that we will look into, but most government bond trackers might not cover a more specific investment exclusion. It is relatively hard to assess the sustainability of a bond issued by a government if it is not specifically a sustainable or green bond (Sweden and other countries have or are in the process of issuing green bonds).

One way of thinking about government bonds is to buy bonds of governments that generally show a care for the environment, societal justice, and sustainability. This involves many European governments in particular. You could use sustainability ratings of governments around the world to pick the bonds you want to invest in.

One way of doing that is to look at the RobecoSAM ESG[30] scores for countries. In 2021 the top 5 were:

1. Finland
2. Sweden
3. Denmark
4. Norway
5. Iceland

Even in those countries there are contradictions as for example Norway is a major exporter of oil. However, these scores look at a variety of metrics, such as Environmental Risk and Status, but also the political situation and the equality of its population as well as social wellbeing. Individuals in these countries also still have a too high CO_2 footprint per person compared to the 2t CO_{2eq} per person that we need to achieve in order to meet our climate targets. However, it is important to note that our global system is based on fossil fuels and therefore it will be hard if not impossible to find a government bond that is truly 100% sustainable. The exception is Bhutan, which is one of the only carbon negative countries in the world, meaning that it emits less than it off-sets through for example its forests.[31] It seems to be impossible thought for the average retail investor to invest in a government bond issued by Bhutan at the time of writing this.

Another way is to buy bonds that are earmarked for sustainable investments. Several governments have and will issue green bonds with such a goal in mind. Sweden for example issued its first green bond in 2020.[32] It is however unclear as of now if and how these bonds will be available to the average retail investor.

Economic Impact

Government bonds are a stable investment asset as most governments are some of the most reliable institutions in the world. Governments could also print more money to meet their debt payments through the central banks. Therefore, there is an understanding that the risk of not being repaid in a government bond is relatively low and one should expect to receive back one's money when a government bond matures.

A rising interest rate will cause the value of your bond to fall as bond rates are inversely proportional to interest rates in the market. So, in that scenario, it's better to invest somewhere else. There is also a high chance that rising inflation will cause the value of your bond to fall. If the rate of inflation rises over the coupon rate of your bond, then your investment will lose your money in real terms. Governments can print money if needed, but too big an increase in the money supply in a short period will lead to a decrease in the face value of money and therefore an overall loss in a bond as the bond's nominal value does not change.

There are short- (<5 years), mid- (5-10 years) and long-term (10+ years) bonds you can invest in, and you want to make sure that you are diversifying your investment across those types. Generally, when investing in government bonds it makes sense to take a longer-term view and focus on mid- and long-term bonds, but this also depends on your risk appetite. For example, if your safety is a top priority you might want to sacrifice some return in exchange for higher stability and a lower risk of loss in short-term bonds. However, if you have a higher risk tolerance and can wait a longer time until you get your investment back you can take on more risk for the higher returns available in long-term bonds.

Bonds

Rating

Liquidity

Long-term bonds themselves are highly illiquid. But by investing in funds that invest in bonds you actually can get the same liquidity as with any other equity fund.

Additionality

Government bonds are relatively low impact if they are not ear-marked for specific causes.

Environment

Government bonds are very broad and low impact if they are not ear-marked for specific causes.

Social

It is hard to be clear on what the social impact of a government bond is if the bond is not specific. But as some of infrastructure projects could be for the common good, the social impact is slightly higher than the environmental one.

Transparency

With government bonds you have quite a bad visibility on what you are financing.

Effort

Investments in bonds are as time consuming as investing in any other type of fund.

Risk

Bonds can be seen as one of the lowest risk assets. That is reflected in their return however, which often is relatively small.

Return

Government bonds in the past have returned on average 5-6% p.a. over the long term according to Morningstar. [33]

Practical Examples

Many investors invest in government bonds via professional money managers such as managed funds. Treasuries can be invested in through quite a few mutual funds or exchange-traded funds (ETFs). Most of the ETFs have low fees, around 0.20% and lower.

Some examples are:

USA
- SPDR® Portfolio Long Term Treasury ETF (SPTL)
- iShares 7-10 Year Treasury Bond ETF (IEF)
- iShares 3-7 Year Treasury Bond ETF (IEI)
- iShares 1-3 Year Treasury Bond ETF (SHY)
- SPDR® Bloomberg Barclays 1-3 Month T-Bill ETF (BIL)

Europe
- iShares € Govt Bond 15-30yr UCITS ETF EUR (Dist)
- SSgA SPDR BBG Barclays 15+ Year Gilt UCITS ETF
- Vanguard EUR Eurozone Government Bond UCITS ETF (EUR) Distributing
- Xtrackers II Eurozone Government Bond 15-30 UCITS ETF 1C
- Xtrackers II Eurozone Government Bond 25+ UCITS ETF 1C

Wells Fargo Municipal Sustainability (USA)   **Fee: 0.75%**

Municipal bonds are an asset class well-suited for investing with impact. Why focus on general-obligation bonds issued by wealthy municipalities and states when you can focus on less well-off issuers that have good sustainability credentials and help them finance projects that create social good?

The fund looks for positive environmental or social impact at both the issuer level and the bond's use of proceeds, using these four criteria:

- The bond's proceeds are to be used on a project or activity that offers tangible environmental or social benefits.
- The issuer, through its services or operations, increases or provides new benefits to the environment or society.
- The issuer or the bond's proceeds address an underserved population group.
- The issuer or bond attains a positive third-party ESG rating.

Lord Abbett Climate Focused Bond (USA)   Fee: 0.45 – 0.65%

Lord Abbett Climate Focused Bond offers investors exposure to medium-term bonds along with a positive impact on the climate. The fund invests in issuers (companies or governments) that are involved in the provision of clean energy, energy efficiency, sustainable transportation, clean water, resource management, or low-carbon solutions. It avoids issuers with poor ESG ratings and those involved in fossil fuel, unless the actual bond being purchased is a green or climate-aligned bond with the use of proceeds going to finance positive climate-related projects.

Corporate Bond ETFs

When an investor is investing in corporate bonds, they are lending money to corporations for a certain number of years. The mechanism is the same as with government bonds, meaning that investors receive interest payments at regular intervals, while the face value of the bond remains unchanged, and the amortization is paid off in a lump-sum in the end of the term.

Environmental and Social Impact

As with equity, the environmental impact of corporate bonds depends on what you invest in as you have the freedom to choose and pick companies that fit your investment focus.

An investment in a corporate bond is often more transparent than in government bonds as you are picking a certain company (or fund) with a particular business profile or focus. You could for example choose to buy a corporate bond that is used by a solar company to install further solar projects with the capital. There is still some unclarity to the exact usage of your capital, but it is definitely improved.

One element to consider in the sustainability of corporate bonds is that - as with government bonds - you will likely invest in these bonds via a fund such as an ETF. This means that at the end of the day, you will have to do the same work as with picking any other actively managed fund. You want a fund that has positive and negative screening criteria.

You want to ensure that the restrictions for the fund's investments are aligned with your values and focus on sustainable alternatives without possible loopholes that allow them to invest otherwise. You should check their investment portfolio (if possible) and the companies they currently are invested in as that gives you an idea what they fund might invest in the future. If you find companies that you do not believe should be in a sustainable fund, avoid investing in that fund.

This information you can often find on the fund's data sheet under sections such as selection criteria. You will also find the assets under management on such a sheet, which shows you the top investments taken by the fund.

Economic Impact

Corporate bonds tend to provide a better return because they present more risk than other bond types. Purchasing government bonds presents a better chance to have a full repayment over their lifetime. In 2015, German-backed government bonds had an interest rate of -0.05%. Corporate bonds with a 7- to 10-year maturity were yielding over 3% at the same time.

You can purchase corporate bonds through public offers or security exchanges. These are referred to as the primary market and secondary market for bonds respectively. Many of these bonds, including private ones, can be sold on an exchange after they have been issued.

If the issuer of a corporate bond goes out of business, then it is possible for the investor to lose their money and the option to receive the intended interest payments. That's a significant risk factor when compared to the bonds that a government issues with a higher credit rating. Since a government can raise taxes to fulfil its obligations, the lower returns are sometimes worth the reduction of risk because of this issue.

There is a high chance that rising inflation will cause the real value of the interest payments to fall. If the rate of inflation rises over the coupon rate of your bond, then your investment will lose your money in real terms.

	Growth	Inflation
Rising	25% OF RISK Equities Commodities Corporate Credit EM Credit	25% OF RISK IL Bonds Commodities EM Credit
Falling	25% OF RISK Nominal Bonds IL Bonds	25% OF RISK Equities Nominal Bonds

MARKET EXPECTATIONS

Figure 6 - Overview of effects of market conditions on bonds

From a portfolio perspective, corporate bonds are good for market conditions that show growth and positive market signals.

Furthermore, bonds are not designed to increase in value during the time they are held. Although some may increase in value (or decrease) on the open market due to changing economic conditions, the goal of a bond is to provide structured interest payments while returning the principal to the investor over time.

Bonds

Rating

Liquidity

Funds investing in corporate bonds have a high liquidity, while investing yourself into a specific corporate bond is having a set term and therefore lower liquidity.

Additionality

Depending on the company or fund you choose the impact can be comparable to actively managed equity funds. Additionality can be slightly higher as these bonds are providing additional capital to the company, while most shares purchases are not resulting in new capital for the company.

Environment

Depending on the company or fund you choose the impact can be comparable to actively managed equity funds.

Social

As you are investing in corporations, this is similar to the equity assets and actively managed equity funds.

Transparency

Investing in corporate bond ETFs does add a slight layer of in-transparency. This can be increased by investing in corporate bonds directly.

Effort

Investing in corporate bond ETFs is similar to equity ETFs, therefore partially automatable and requires less work of balancing than investing in corporate bonds directly.

Risk

Corporate bonds have a higher risk than government bonds as they rely on a smaller institution to pay back the investment. The final risk here depends to a huge extent on the maturity of the company issuing the bond.

Return

Similar to the risk, the return depends on how mature the company issuing it is. For the funds mentioned later the returns have been around the 2% p.a. mark.

Practical Examples

It generally seems a lot harder to find corporate bonds that match the sustainability criteria and are investable for retail investors. Below are two possible examples, even though their fit in this sub-category can be discussed.

Triodos Euro Bond Impact Fund (EU)   **Fee: 1.26%**

Triodos Euro Bond Impact Fund aims to generate positive impact and stable income from a concentrated portfolio of investment-grade, euro-denominated bonds issued by listed companies, and semi-public institutions and EU member state governments. This is therefore not a "pure" corporate bond but has elements of it in the overall exposure and therefore could provide a good addition to a portfolio. The fee, however, is high and could reduce the return to investors.

Lord Abbett Climate Focused Bond (USA)   **Fee: 0.45 – 0.65%**

As this is the same fund as before, you can see an overview in the previous chapter.

The fact that government bonds are mixed with corporate bonds in these two instruments make them less transparent than they could be and makes it harder to assess the real sustainable impact they have in reality.

Lannebo Sustainable Corporate Bond (SWE)   **Fee: 0.9%**

Lannebo Sustainable Corporate Bond is an actively managed fund that invests mainly in corporate bonds issued by companies in the Nordics and parts of Europe. They focus on four themes:

- Green Bonds
- Better Environment
- Healthier Lifestyle
- Sustainable Society

Corporate Debt Crowdfunding

To circumvent the issue of finding suitable sustainable corporate bonds for retail investors we can turn to crowdinvesting/crowdfunding.

As with equity, debt crowdfunding is a new way of investing. Different from equity however, you are lending money to a company or a project to achieve a very specific result. The investment amount is often relatively small and can start at just a few dozen EUR/USD, which makes this accessible to a lot of people.

As mentioned before, you should never put all your assets in one basket. This is particularly true when it comes to early-stage debt, often called venture debt. Depending on what you decide to invest most often corporate debt crowdfunding should be a small part of your portfolio - more on that later.

This sub-asset class can take many different shapes, anything from traditional stocks in a company to shares in a project and profit sharing on a particular sub-part of a venture.

Environmental Impact

With the risk of repetition, the environmental impact of providing debt to borrowers depends on which opportunities you decide to invest in. You can invest in a wide variety of companies, making it hard to give a precise overview, but we will go through some examples later.

You can invest in a specific purpose (or use of funds), helping you to know with more clarity what your money is being used for. This gives you the transparency needed to assess the sustainability and impact of your investments.

This is a very active part of your potential portfolio as you are supporting a new venture or project. The impact your money is having on those early-stage companies and projects is generally bigger than in established companies as you are really helping to get something new off the ground. Without your (and others') investment the company or project would either not exist or have a much higher risk of failing. Therefore, you are clearly setting a positive additional action by investing in sustainable early-stage companies and projects.

Some of the key investment criteria you should consider are:

> **Replacing existing goods or services with a more sustainable alternative**
>
> We have a throw-away society today due to products being one-use items and not being recyclable. As most goods at the moment are produced unsustainably there is a huge market opportunity for companies to innovate and replace materials such as plastic with more sustainable alternatives that are reusable, recyclable, or biodegradable. This will lead to closed loops and less waste, which in turn will reduce the need to produce new materials from raw resources, such as plastic from oil.

> **New business model with a more effective use of goods or services**
>
> Similarly, we live in a society where people own items that they hardly or never use. One way to combat this issue is to invest in companies that offer new alternatives to using items, such as sharing them among more people. There have been several examples already, such as Airbnb (instead of building new hotels) or car sharing apps (instead of owning your own car). We also need to increase the re-use of goods that are not being used by their owner anymore and might be thrown away otherwise. This includes good second-hand stores that refurbish items and make it as easy to buy used products as it is currently with new ones.

> **Using waste for new products or services**
>
> A lot of the waste of our society that cannot be reused could be used for new purposes if it were recycled. Any company that has identified a sustainable use of waste enables us getting closer to closed loops and a more effective use of our resources.

> **Companies that operate in a key sustainability sector**
>
> Besides companies that are innovating new business models or new and better use of resources, we need more companies doing the right thing in key sectors. Reducing our impact on the climate and on nature in these sectors will reap major benefits for our society's sustainability. This includes renewable energy production, sustainable transportation, and sustainable agriculture.

Social Impact

The social impact of this type of corporate bond can be substantial. Many socially responsible businesses are raising money in this way as they often have a hard time accessing funding via other more traditional routes. Often more commercial investors don't see the value in the companies that provide social impact and don't see it as a viable business case with a big enough market. However, social injustice and the under-served communities are a market of over 1 billion people globally, representing a huge business opportunity.

Due to the catalytic nature of your investment in this asset class and it being an active part of your portfolio, it drives a real positive change in society. Be it solar energy for people living in energy poverty, education for underprivileged parts of society or clean drinking water projects for emerging countries. All of these have a tremendous social impact as they target to reduce inequality through inclusive business models.

We live in times where positive social impact and for-profit business models are not necessarily opposites any longer. As more and more companies see business opportunities in serving the so-called bottom of the pyramid (living with an income of less than 8 USD per day) these people get increased access to services and opportunities not available before. This can help elevate them out of poverty.

Companies can have a social impact in different ways:

1. By providing services not available previously to underprivileged parts of society. This could be education, better money management or access to information such as news or weather reports for small-scale farmers.

2. By providing new and often better paid job opportunities to underprivileged parts of society. Important is that the new job opportunities do not exploit people and also improve working conditions and rights for this part of the population.

3. By providing important infrastructure that improves life quality. This could be access to clean electricity through solar power or technology to increase farming output such as water pumps.

Economic Impact

This way of investing in corporate bonds has a potential higher return, but at the same time the companies raising debt this way are often in the early stage and there is no additional upside compared to equity. Bond investments are not designed to increase in value during the time they are held. Their goal is to provide structured interest payments while returning the principal to the investor over time. Equity on the other hand has the advantage of being able to multiply its valuation many-fold in such early-stage companies.

The upside is that you have many options to invest in due to the vast amount of companies raising capital this way and the numerous investment platforms allowing you to invest in these bonds. This in turn gives you many options to diversify your portfolio and reduce your risk. This is particularly important in a category such as this one with increased risks due to the early stage of many of the borrowers.

The liquidity of most debt investments is relatively low with many debt instruments having a lifetime of 3 to 5 years or even longer. If the platform you are investing in does not have a well-functioning and liquid secondary market, it is close to impossible to liquidate your investments if you end up in a situation where you need more capital or cash for an urgent purpose.

It also takes more time to assess investment opportunities in this category as you have to look at more detailed information per investment and as you probably want to spread your risk as many investments as possible. This leads to you not being able to invest a big portion of your investment portfolio in this category if you don't have the time to continuously assess new opportunities.

There is a chance that rising inflation will cause the real value of the bonds' interest payments to fall. If the rate of inflation rises over the coupon rate of your bond, then your investment will lose your money in real terms. From a portfolio perspective, these bonds are good for market conditions that show growth and positive market signals.

Overall, it should be said that due to this sub-segment's higher risk nature, it should not take a big portion of your investment portfolio, in particular if you are closer to retirement and cannot bear bigger losses.

 Bonds

Rating

Liquidity

Investing directly in corporate bonds means that you will have to wait for the maturity of the bond to be paid out.

Additionality

Corporate bonds in this category have a high additionality as the capital raised goes directly to the company and its operations, instead of to investors.

Environment

Choosing the corporate bonds, yourself means you can choose companies with a high impact.

Social

Choosing the corporate bonds, yourself means you can choose companies with a high impact.

Transparency

Investing directly in corporate bonds gives you a higher control over what you are financing compared to ETFs. This is enhanced by the fact that most of these types of corporate bonds have a specific use of funds, increasing their transparency.

Effort

Investing directly comes with the downside of more time being necessary to manage your investments. You will need to re-invest your money and find corporate bonds that fit your investment criteria.

Risk

Most companies raising bonds in this category are relatively early stage. If the bond is ear-marked for a project, its repayment can often hinge on that specific use of funds, increasing the risks of something going wrong and a default happening.

Return

Most bonds discussed here have returns of 5-7% p.a.

Practical Examples

You will see that there is a buffet of debt investment platforms out there. You need to decide which platform you want to invest on first. You can pick as many of course and below is a list that gives you a rough overview of what exists.

After you have identified on which platforms you want to start, you need to decide what kind of companies or projects you want to invest in on those platforms.

Bettervest (EU)   bettervest.com

Total Invested	# Investments
24MEUR+	120+ projects

Bettervest was launched in 2012 to finance energy efficiency projects run by citizens. Nowadays, the platform offers projects in many different areas, all sustainability related and gives a return of about 7%.

Energise Africa (UK/EU)   energiseafrica.com

Total Invested	# Investments	Min
33MGBP	200+	25 GBP

Energise Africa, similarly to Trine, offers debt investment opportunities into solar energy companies in Africa.

GLS Crowd (EU)   https://www.gls-crowd.de/

Total Invested	Total Invested
20MEUR+	20MEUR+

GLS Crowd focuses on providing debt to sustainable companies. It works in partnership with GLS Bank, operating in Germany.

Goparity   **Goparity.com**

Total Invested	# Investments	Min
36 MEUR	357+	250 EUR

Goparity is an impact finance and investment app that empowers people and companies to actively contribute to the United Nation's Sustainable Development Goals.

---

klimja (EU)   **Klimja.com**

Total Invested	# Investments	Min
6.25 MEUR	2,900+	250 EUR

Klimja is the crowd investing platform for climate protection and climate change adaptation measures in developing countries. The platform finances projects that meet certain sustainability criteria (social and ecological standards and guidelines), which contribute to the reduction of greenhouse gases and sustainable development.

Lumo (FR/EU)   **lumo-france.com**

Total Invested	# Investments	Min
176MEUR	200+	50 EUR

Lumo is offering debt investment opportunities in renewable energy projects, mainly in France.

Rockets (EU) 　　　　**https://rockets.investments**

Total Invested	# Investments	Min
195MEUR	300+	250 EUR

Rockets (and its sub-arm Green Rockets in particular) specializes in investing in sustainable start-ups. You can find anything from solar energy to sustainable food on their website.

Trine (EU) 　　　　**trine.com**

Total Invested	# Investments	Min
90MEUR+	100+	25 EUR

On Trine you can provide loans for solar energy providers in Africa. You have a clear impact with your investment as you provide electricity to people that live off the grid currently and you replace fossil fuels with renewable energy.
(Note: I am one of the founders of Trine)

RE Royalties (CAN) 　　　　**reroyalties.com**

Total Invested	# Investments	Min
20MCAD+	80+	5000 CAD

RE Royalties issues a green bond that invests in specific renewable energy projects in Canada, the USA and Europe, including solar, wind and hydro power plants. They currently offer a 6% return to investors with a bond tenor of 5 years and quarterly payments. This investment opportunity is only available to Canadian investors as of now.

Microfinance

Originally an idea by Grameen Foundation founder Muhammad Yunus, microfinance originated in Bangladesh in the mid-1970s as an alternative form of banking in which banks make small loans to the poorer parts of the local population.

Its aim is that motivated and disciplined poor people can get out of poverty by having access to funding—even small amounts— to establish their own businesses. With access to finance, such "micro-entrepreneurs" can build their businesses, pay back the money, and provide for themselves and their families.

A typical example would be a woman who borrows $50 to buy chickens in order to sell eggs to other members of her community. As her chicken's breed, she can sell more eggs, and at some point, she can even sell chicks. She pays back the money and has resolved a perhaps desperate financial situation, while the community benefits from an additional source of nutritious food.

Environmental Impact

Microfinance has shown over the last three decades that when poor people are given opportunities to earn a living, they have little or no need to use their surrounding natural resources to shelter or feed themselves. Many of the financial institutions doing microfinance also subscribe to sustainability as one of the preconditions for lending money. Others support sustainable businesses by giving lower interest rates to borrowers with sustainability-oriented business plans.

In emerging economies, access to affordable renewable energy, safe water and agricultural inputs can be particularly valuable due to a lack of infrastructure. The story about a village that had no access to electricity until it was connected to solar power is one example, but there are many other opportunities to invest in. Some include certified agricultural and forestry products, water storage systems, rainwater harvesting systems, drip irrigation, high-quality & certified agricultural inputs and - of course - solar energy.

"Green Microfinance" seeks to address these opportunities, by providing low- or moderate-income individuals with loans to help them procure and set up "green" or environmentally friendly products and technology. Microenterprises have been very popular in Asia, with the Asian Developmental Bank stating that they account for more than 60 per cent of all enterprises and 50 per cent of paid employment.[34]

But it also must be said that some microentrepreneurs operate in business activities that have negative environmental impacts. These impacts can range from small-scale industrial pollution to land degradation by agriculture. The range of impacts differs between urban and rural regions and is caused by many factors. Here are some examples on how small businesses can damage the environment:

- Agriculture — crop, and cattle grazing
- Metal work and electroplating
- Forest product collectors — including fuel wood and non-timber forest products
- Pesticide and chemical manufacturers
- Small-scale mining
- Textiles and dyeing operations
- Automobile and motor repair
- Wood processors — carpentry and construction
- Transportation — rickshaws, taxis, and small buses

Many rural enterprises involve cattle and crop agriculture — these have effects on soil quality and biodiversity. Soil erosion from agriculture is a major environmental impact as it affects the productive capacity of the land and water quality. When land's productive capacity is reduced it has an immediate effect on food security.

Rural farmers also get loans to buy pesticides. Improper use of those pesticides and fertilizers can have a major negative effect on the environment. Nutrient and pesticide runoff affect the water quality. And many of these businesses do create dangerous waste by-products that often get discarded in an indiscriminate fashion since there are no adequate facilities and there is a lack of regulation and enforcement.

It should be noted that most informal businesses do not cause significant harm to the environment and often can be very beneficial (Pallen 1997). Many of the harmful effects can also be mitigated or reduced without threatening the viability and growth of these micro-businesses. In many cases increased efficiency with the input and reduction of waste is a win-win since it saves businesses money and increases profits while reducing the effects on the climate.

Overall, it is important to pick a microfinance investment option that clearly outlines the focus on sustainability. This can either be done by picking the direct investments yourself or by thoroughly reading up on the fund's focus. More on that in the practical examples.

Social Impact

As you are providing loans directly or indirectly to individuals in emerging markets, you can have a tremendous social impact that would not have been possible without your money. It is one of the most promising approaches to elevate people out of poverty in a sustainable manner. It is however not all straight-forward and there are some important details to consider.

Depending on who you talk to about microfinance, it is either the silver bullet to solve global poverty and should be a basic human right, or it's taking advantage of the global poor that only leads to more inequality and more resources in the hands of the wealthy. A long line of studies has been unable to conclusively prove the point for either side fully.

The major issue with microfinance institutions (MFI) is often the interest rate that is being charged to the borrowers, often families or small businesses. These can be in staggering ranges of above 70%, sometimes even 100% or more. This does indeed seem questionable and none of us in the western countries would take on a loan with such interest rates. However, it must be said that many people borrow funds for a relatively short period of time, for example a few weeks only. And the operation in these emerging markets is often difficult and not as simple as in many western countries.

Another metric that can be interesting to look at is the return on equity (ROE) of MFIs. Generally speaking, the ROE should be questioned if it is above high return stocks such as Google. That would put the number around the 20% mark. And there are some MFIs that generate ROEs above this mark, therefore making a sizable profit off of their clients, often people living at the bottom of the pyramid. There is clearly a potential moral issue here that each investor needs to discuss with themselves and then decide if you want to go ahead with this investment or not.

Looking through available research on MFIs shows a range of evidence that microfinance programs can increase incomes and lift families out of poverty. Access to microfinance can improve children's nutrition and increase their school enrolment rates, among many other outcomes. However, it depends heavily on which bank and program one looks at as they use different methods and have different customers. Which makes it impossible to generally say that microfinance is the holy grail for social impact.

A study of villages in Bangladesh showed the positive impact of microfinance on those communities.[35] The study surveyed over 1,500 households in 87 villages done three times in 20 years, concluding that microfinance "increases (the microentrepreneurs') income and spending, the amount of work available to them, non-land holdings, net assets, as well as the education of boys and girls."

The impacts of microfinance can for example be any of the following:

- An improvement of living conditions for the borrower and their family
- An empowerment and emancipation of women
- An increased level of income
- An increased stability of income
- A development from an informal economy to a formal economy

What is debated is if microfinance leads to more than an increase in income and business activity. Both education and health care are not clearly improved by microfinance when looking at the available research. For example, a microloan might help a family start a business, but if a single family member suddenly falls ill, they might be unable to keep their business going—and will probably spend all the money they have on emergency health care. Which in the end does not help them out of poverty, but rather puts them back into poverty.

In order to prevent such things from happening a number of additional measures need to be in place that are not only microfinance. Such measures could be social security programs by the governments, free basic healthcare, and education as well as unemployment insurance. Fully elevating people out of poverty is a complex task and microfinance is not a silver bullet to it, but a possible puzzle piece.

Economic Impact

Most microfinance services report high repayment rates and low default rates, as the finance is often used for productive uses that increase the income of the borrower, often families and in particular women. This helps to reduce the risk of such loans to a level where it makes economic sense to invest in.

Investments in microfinance are not directly correlated to the global markets. As most of the borrowers live in economies that are slightly isolated from movements in more developed countries and stock exchanges, your investments will continue repaying even in a stock market crash as long as the individual borrowers are able to repay their loan. This makes microfinance a good diversification investment. Even if your local economy is in a downward cycle and other investments are performing poorly, microfinance could still be earning your returns.

Most investments in microfinance are similar to bonds in the sense that they have a fixed interest rate. This means that in inflationary investment periods, microfinance investments are not off setting any losses resulted by the value loss of the underlying currency.

Some of these investment opportunities are on separate platforms, increasing once again the complexity of your investment portfolio and the time it takes to manage it. As on some platforms these loans also tend to be quite short-term you will have to spend some work reinvesting your returns. This should be considered from an economic perspective when making the investment choices as it will increase your workload connected to that portion of your investment portfolio.

Rating

Liquidity

This investment has a relatively good liquidity as most microfinance loans are short-term loans.

Additionality

Investing in microfinance gives finance to people that often lack access to capital. Therefore, the additionality is substantial here.

Environment

As most of microfinance is used for small-scale entrepreneurs the impact is often more on the neutral side.

Social

Giving people finance to grow their business and hopefully escape poverty is a great vision. Microfinance falls short of achieving this vision sometimes but should still be seen as a net-positive impact. Therefore, the slight down-rating to 4.

Transparency

Most of the time it is clear what your money will be used for as you are providing single loans to individuals.

Effort

You will have to do more manual work in the investment process than with stocks, and often have to reinvest your returns yourself.

Risk

Providing loans to individuals in different countries/continents with close to zero banking background can be seen as very risky.

Return

This depends how you invest, but on average you can assume a 5-7% p.a. return on your microfinance investments.

Practical Examples

There are several ways to invest in microfinance and the list below provides an overview of places you can do so. It covers mainly investment offers that are accessible to people with the smallest pocket (e.g. low investment sizes) and companies that seem to do the right thing in terms of sustainability.

Most microfinance funds are unfortunately not easily accessible for retail investors. There are ways to invest in a microfinance fund by Triodos, but it seems to have become harder lately as it is only available via financial advisors.

<table>
<tr><td>Triodos Microfinance Fund (EU)</td><td>https://www.triodos-im.com/funds/individual/nl</td></tr>
</table>

Total Invested
460 million EUR

Triodos operates a fund that solely targets microfinance institutions across the world. They work with over 90 of such institutions across more than 40 countries in Africa, Asia, Eastern Europe, and Latin America. The fund provides both equity and debt to these borrowers.

Investing in this Triodos fund has become increasingly difficult. As of the date of this writing you can only invest through a financial intermediary in the UK as an individual. If you do not have one you could find a green and ethical advisor via the Ethical Investment Association in the UK (http://https//ethicalinvestment.org.uk/financial-adviser/).

There are relatively high fees on the fund. There is an initial charge of 3% when you invest your funds and an ongoing charge of over 2%. With average returns in the past years being around 3.8% there is not much left for you as an investor after paying these charges.

Lendahand (EU)   https://www.lendahand.com/en-EU

Total Invested	Jobs Created	#Projects
170 million EUR	12,000	3,000

Founded in 2013, Lendahand is a for-profit company that is on a mission to eradicate poverty through crowdfunding. The platform gives investors in Europe the chance to invest in people and businesses in emerging markets that do not have access to the capital they desperately need to function.

The financing goes to SMEs and financial institutions that have a track record and proven business model, which in turn are able to create new jobs and improve their local economies. It is not direct microfinance, meaning you provide a loan to an individual or family, but rather through an intermediary through which your money will be used for a certain use case.

An example of a loan given through the platform is Phillip Bank Plc that raised money to finance small local entrepreneurs. In one of their loans, they raised finance for several entrepreneurs:

- Chhery Sokkea (28), a cassava farmer, who needed a new loan to purchase farm items through working capital.
- Tep Chet (40), a bamboo seller in his community who needed a loan to purchase more bamboo to resale.
- Heng Pheara (28) who has a vehicle repair shop and needed a loan to buy vehicle repair supplies to stock in his store.
- Chhon Navy (30) who has a phone shop and needed a loan to invest in a Tuk Tuk service in his community.
- Sok Kimheang (48), a traditional spagitti khmer seller, needed to take a loan for her son to buy a new car for his Taxi provider service.
- Sman Noutsoupfiyany (28), a shoes seller in a market in Phnom Penh, Cambodia. She needed more working capital to buy more stock.

Oikocredit (EU & US)   **https://www.oikocredit.coop/en**

Total Invested	Partners	Investors
1,100 million EUR	520+	48,000+

Oikocredit is a social impact investor, operating globally as a cooperative. They were founded in 1975 and have since then invested in positive impact with the capital of private and institutional investors. Their focus is on investments in the areas of financial inclusion, agriculture, and renewable energy.

In agriculture, Oikocredit finances rural microfinance and producer organizations, for example agricultural cooperatives, with the aim of supporting local economies and stronger communities. In the renewable energy segment Oikocredit focuses on solar, wind, small hydropower, biomass, and energy-efficiency projects. And in the microfinance area, they provide finance directly to microfinance institutions (MFIs) and banks that support small and medium enterprises (SMEs).

Oikocredit might not be as transparent as Lendahand and other crowdfunding platforms, but at the same time they manage your funds while having a very clear mission and vision statement that clearly defines what they can invest in.

To invest with Oikocredit, you can simply go to their homepage and via "Invest in Oikocredit" pick your country. Individuals and organizations can invest by buying "depository receipts". These give you the financial rights of an Oikocredit co-operative shareholder without direct membership. You can invest in either euros or pounds sterling, with a minimum investment being €200 or £150 and no maximum. Investors get a maximum 2% dividend, paid once a year. This has been paid every year since 1989, two years when it was 1% and recently due to the effect of COVID on the Oikocredit portfolio.

If you want to withdraw your funds you can do so at any time. There are also no annual management charges, commissions, and other charges.

Kiva (Global)   **kiva.org**

Total Invested	# of loans	People Reached
1,600 million USD	2.3 million	5 million

First and most importantly, Kiva is not an investment platform. The reason they are mentioned here is that they have a substantial footprint in the microfinance space today and could be part of your philanthropic capital.

Kiva is a non-profit organization based out of San Francisco, California that allows people to lend money to low-income entrepreneurs and students. Kiva's mission is "to expand financial access to help underserved communities thrive." Since 2005, Kiva has raised over $1.6 billion, with a repayment rate of 96. As an investor, you do not receive interest on the money lent.

Kiva works with a network of field partners to manage the loans on the ground. These partners are often either microfinance institutions, social impact businesses, or non-profit organizations. The final borrowers pay interest on most loans to the field partners, and the field partners are charged small fees by Kiva. Kiva sustains itself through grants, loans, and donations from their users, corporations, and national institutions. This means that 100% of your capital is directly on-lent to the borrower, without any charges by kiva themselves.

Not all loans on Kiva are sustainable as some finance the use of fossil fuels or chemical fertilizers, but they have their own sub-category of green loans that are only to sustainable business and ideas. These can be cleaner and safer forms of energy, green agriculture, transport, and recycling.

V – Portfolio Suggestions

So far you have seen a (non-exhaustive) list of possibilities for investments, some more and some less sustainable. Now the really tricky question is, how should you split your capital in all or some of these assets?

The answer is unfortunately not as simple as you and I might wish. As it turns out, the world is relatively complex and there are no clear silver bullets. With the following sections I give you three suggestions for splitting your capital in the mentioned categories.

The major underlying principle of all portfolios is that diversity is the crucial element to keeping your portfolio healthy - like in nature. This should therefore always be your guiding principle for investments, even if you choose a different capital allocation than presented later on.

Bob Rice, the Chief Investment Strategist of the investment bank Tangent Capital, stated that more traditional 60/40 portfolios (60% equity, 40% bonds) are not going to continue growing at the same rate as in the 80s and 90s, but rather at around 2% per year. He argued himself that investors should look more at private equity, commodities such as precious metals, collectibles, and venture capital.[36]

He stated that "due to high equity valuations; monetary policies that have never previously been used; increased risks in bond funds; and low prices in the commodities markets" these traditional 60/40 portfolios have been underperforming. "You cannot invest in one future anymore; you have to invest in multiple futures," Rice said. Rice also states to look at different alternative assets in instead of bonds, such as the royalties, debt instruments from emerging markets, and debt and equity funds.

It must be noted that this is not representative of the view of mainstream finance though. But then again, mainstream finance has not done the shift to sustainable investments (yet).

Generally, for retail investors like yourself investing in all these assets is difficult and was impossible before. But thanks to new ways of investing, there are possibilities now to do so. We have highlighted many of these investment assets Rice mentioned and now we just have to decide how much to invest in each.

There are three portfolio allocations I want to highlight. The idea behind them is how much impact you want to make and how much risk you want to take. The first suggestion is arguably not moving the needle much in terms of the sustainability of your investments while the other two suggestions are more aggressive, but also riskier.

Below is an overview of all portfolios and the individual ratings. You will find a table in the Appendix with the ratings in decimal forms instead.

	Low Risk Portfolio	Medium Risk Portfolio	High-Risk Portfolio
Liquidity	★★★★⯨	★★★★☆	★★★⯨☆
Additionality	★★☆☆☆	★★⯨☆☆	★★★★☆
Environment	★★☆☆☆	★★★☆☆	★★★★☆
Social	★★⯨☆☆	★★★☆☆	★★★★☆
Transparency	★★☆☆☆	★★★☆☆	★★★★☆
Time	★★★⯨☆	★★★⯨☆	★★★⯨☆
Risk	★★★★⯨	★★★★☆	★★⯨☆☆
Return	★★★⯨☆	★★★⯨☆	★★★⯨☆

I believe though that even if you pick the least sustainable option mentioned here, you will still make an impact as you are moving some capital away from the fossil fuel industry and sending a clear signal to the financial and corporate sector that change is needed

Low Risk/Impact Portfolio

Liquidity	★★★★⯪
Additionality	★★☆☆☆
Environment	★★☆☆☆
Social	★★⯪☆☆
Transparency	★★☆☆☆
Effort	★★★⯪☆
Risk	★★★★⯪
Return	★★★⯪☆

Mind Your Money

First is the traditional All-Season portfolio approach with high-risk diversification, with some slight modifications. This is based on suggestions from major investors such as Ray Dalio and therefore likely the most balanced portfolio when it comes to risk.

This portfolio suits a person that wants to ensure a successful investment strategy while making such a portfolio slightly more sustainable in terms of its environmental and social impact. Which leads us to the main disadvantage of this portfolio - it does not have many active sustainable investment assets. For example, reforestation projects are not included here and also the exposure to start-up companies through equity crowdfunding is being avoided as these have higher risk profiles that scrutinize the All-Season approach.

With that in mind the split should somewhat be similar to the following.

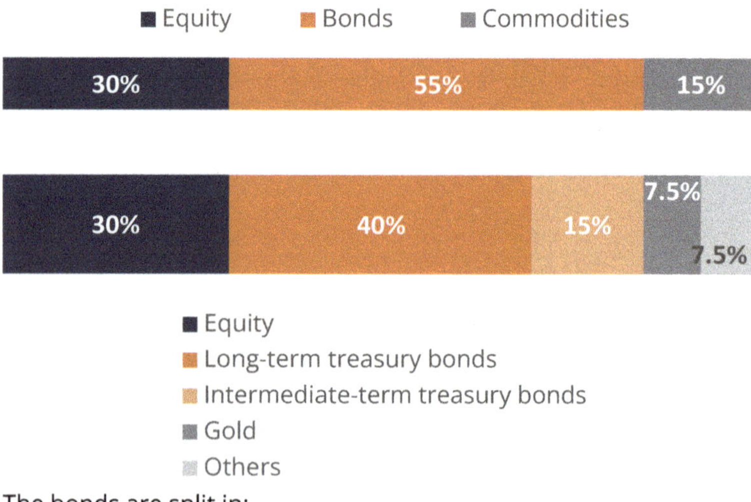

The bonds are split in:
- 40% long-term treasury bonds (20-25 years)
- 15% intermediate-term treasury bonds (7-10 years)

and the commodities consist of:
- 7.5% gold
- 7.5% others

In each of the sub-categories you want to ensure additional adequate diversification. As for example investing all your equity allocation only in one stock would make even an All-Season portfolio quite volatile and frankly pointless due to the concentration risk. The level of sub-diversification depends on how much work you want to spend on managing your investments, in particular the re-balancing element of it.

30% Equity	
A suggestion is to split your capital amongst individual stocks you and funds with an sustainable investment agenda.	
5% **Stocks**	You can invest 5% of your total capital into stocks such as Tesla. This enables you to profit directly from companies that you believe in without paying fees for a fund. The total exposure to stocks depends on your risk appetite but should be limited due to their volatility and heavier workload when it comes to re-balancing each individual stock.
10-15% **Index Funds**	One reason for having a higher exposure to index funds is their low fees. One has to note however the higher your share in index funds is the less actively sustainable your overall portfolio becomes. You might want to lower that down to 10% if you want to allocate a higher percentage to actively managed funds.
10 – 15% **Actively** **managed** **Funds**	Actively managed funds are generally more expensive, but also better in allocating capital to companies that try to make a true difference - and therefore more sustainable. As with index funds, you can vary this percentage up to 15% if you deem the extra costs worth the environmental benefit.

55% Bonds	
40% Long-term Bonds	Similar to equity (and most other assets here) you want to spread these 40% overall exposure to several bond instruments. How much spread you take is in the end up to you and depends on how much time you want to spend on managing this sub-segment. A good place to start would be investing in 4 long-term bonds, 10% in each. They should have a focus on 10+ years.
15% Medium-Term Bonds	For intermediate bonds the suggestion is to spread the 15% among three bonds, up to your liking. They should focus on a 7 to 10 years time horizon.
15% Commodities	
7.5 – 15% Gold	Here 7.5% should be ear-marked for gold, while the remaining 7.5% can be used for other commodities. You could decide to put all 15% into gold, as it simplifies your investment and also gives you a higher exposure to gold. One way to increase sustainability is to buy Fairmined gold or a similar asset, at the very least as a part of your investment.
0 – 7.5% Other	

Example Split

<table>
<tr><td rowspan="15">5%
Stocks</td><td colspan="3" align="center">30% Equity</td></tr>
<tr><td>Share</td><td>Company</td><td>Sector</td></tr>
<tr><td>0.25%</td><td>Tesla</td><td>Clean transport / Electric cars</td></tr>
<tr><td>0.25%</td><td>Vestas</td><td>Renewable Energy / Wind</td></tr>
<tr><td>0.25%</td><td>SunPower Corp</td><td>Renewable Energy / Solar</td></tr>
<tr><td>0.25%</td><td>GreenMobility</td><td>Electric transportation / Car sharing</td></tr>
<tr><td>0.25%</td><td>REC Silicon</td><td>Renewable Energy / Solar</td></tr>
<tr><td>0.25%</td><td>Maxeon Solar Technologies Ltd</td><td>Renewable Energy / Solar</td></tr>
<tr><td>0.25%</td><td>Shimano</td><td>Clean transport / Bike parts</td></tr>
<tr><td>0.25%</td><td>Stericycle</td><td>Waste management / Recycling</td></tr>
<tr><td>0.25%</td><td>Umwelt Bank AG</td><td>Finance / Bank</td></tr>
<tr><td>0.25%</td><td>Ormat Technologies</td><td>Renewable Energy / Geothermal</td></tr>
<tr><td>0.25%</td><td>Kadant</td><td>Waste management / Recycling</td></tr>
<tr><td>0.25%</td><td>East Japan Railway</td><td>Clean transport / Railways</td></tr>
<tr><td>0.25%</td><td>Sims Metal Management</td><td>Waste management / Recycling</td></tr>
<tr><td>0.25%</td><td>Tomra Systems</td><td>Waste management / Recycling</td></tr>
<tr><td>0.25%</td><td>United Natural Foods</td><td>Sustainable food</td></tr>
</table>

0.25%	Acciona	Renewable Energy / Wind & Transport
0.25%	First Solar	Renewable Energy / Solar
0.25%	Iberdrola	Renewable Energy
0.25%	NextEra	Renewable Energy / Solar
0.25%	Brookfield Renewable Partners	Renewable Energy

10% Index Funds	2.5%	First Trust ISE Global Wind Energy Index Fund	Renewable Energy
	2.5%	iShares MSCI Global Impact ETF	Impact
	2.5%	Öhman Etisk Emerging Markets A	Emerging Markets
	2.5%	Öhman Global Marknad Hållbar A	Global
15% Active Funds	5%	CB Save Earth Fund RC	Global Impact
	5%	Triodos Global Equities Impact Fund	Global Impact
	5%	Triodos Renewables Europe Fund	Renewable Energy

55% Bonds		
	Share	**Fund**
15% Medium-term Bonds	10%	SSgA SPDR BBG Barclays 15+ Year Gilt UCITS ETF
	10%	Xtrackers II Eurozone Government Bond 15-30 UCITS ETF 1C
	10%	Xtrackers II Eurozone Government Bond 25+ UCITS ETF 1C
	10%	SSgA SPDR BBG Barclays 15+ Year Gilt UCITS ETF
15% Medium-term Bonds	5%	Invesco Euro Government Bond 5-7 Year UCITS ETF
	5%	Ossiam Euro Government Bonds 3-5 Carbon Reduction - UCITS ETF 1C
	5%	iShares Global Inflation Linked Govt Bond UCITS ETF USD

15% Commodities		
	Share	**Fund**
7.5% Gold	3.75%	Gold on BullionVault
	3.75%	WisdomTree Physical Swiss Gold ETC
7.5% Others	3.75%	Gold on BullionVault
	3.75%	Fairmined Gold via Fairever

Low Risk/Impact Portfolio

Medium Risk/Impact Portfolio

Liquidity	★★★★☆
Additionality	★★⯪☆☆
Environment	★★★☆☆
Social	★★★☆☆
Transparency	★★★☆☆
Effort	★★★⯪☆
Risk	★★★★☆
Return	★★★⯪☆

Mind Your Money

This portfolio does not fully resemble anymore the original All-Season Portfolio idea. That is mainly because there are many other assets being part of the portfolio, in order to add more high risk, but active and high impact assets. The main idea of diversification remains and is an integral part of this portfolio.

This portfolio suits a person that wants to ensure a successful investment strategy while making the most of their portfolio active and high impact regarding climate change. This is one of the major advantages of this portfolio compared to the previous one, but also one of its weaknesses. As you are investing in higher risk assets, the portfolio will be less balanced, and it will be harder to assess the risk spread of your investment. As for example it is hard to assess the volatility of early-stage investments in start-up companies through equity crowdfunding.

The split looks slightly different now from the previous portfolio.

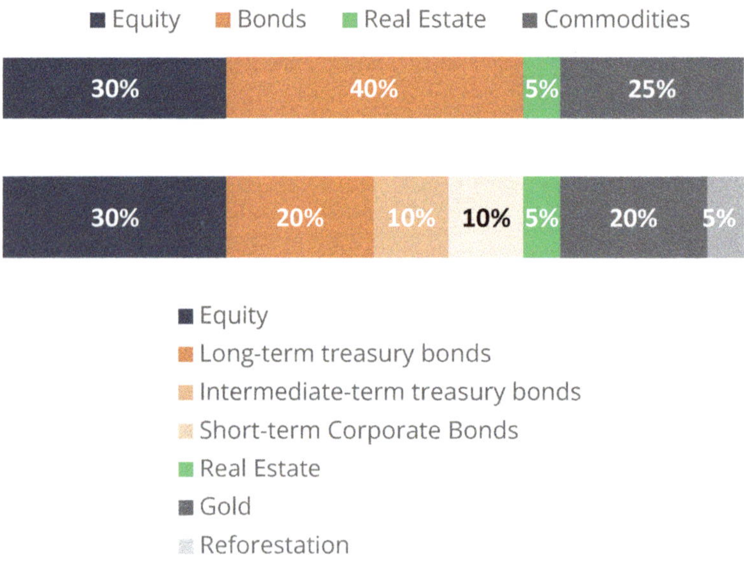

       Medium Risk/Impact Portfolio

The bonds are split in:
- 20% long-term treasury bonds (20-25 years)
- 10% intermediate-term treasury bonds (7-10 years)
- 10% short-term corporate bonds (<3 years)

and the commodities consist of:
- 15-20% gold
- 5 – 10% reforestation
- Small portions of Bitcoin if interested.

In each of the sub-categories you want to ensure additional adequate diversification to spread the risks as much as possible. The level of sub-diversification depends on how much work you want to spend on managing your investments, in particular the re-balancing element of it.

Whatever portion of your capital you have not allocated to an investment class, you want to put in a liquid savings account, preferably with an ethical bank as discussed in the beginning of this book. This enables you to draw down money when needed without affecting your portfolio.

30% Equity	
5 – 10% **Stocks**	You can invest up to 10% of your total capital into stocks such as Tesla. This sub-asset class should be aligned with the early-stage equity exposure, so that combined do not exceed 10%.
0 – 5% **Early-stage** **Companies**	As early-stage companies are often creating real change, this is one of the most active parts of this investment portfolio. As it is a rather risky portion the suggestion is not to invest too high a share of your capital here, but if you deem you can take more risk you can increase this share to a higher level. The ceiling should be 10% to keep the exposure here to a minimum. This sub-asset class should be aligned with the stock exposure, so that combined do not exceed 10%.
5% **Index Funds**	We are reducing index funds slightly to cater for both the increased portion for stocks, but also to increase the sustainability of the portfolio as index funds are the least sustainable part of the equity investment.
15% **Active Funds**	Active funds are also reduced, however not by as much as they are having a higher impact on the sustainability of the portfolio and therefore weigh higher when it comes to prioritizing which part to reduce to accommodate the increase stock and early-stage company portion.

     Medium Risk/Impact Portfolio

<table>
<tr><td colspan="2" align="center">40% Bonds</td></tr>
<tr>
<td align="center">20%
Long-term
Bonds</td>
<td>You want to spread these 20% overall exposure to several bond instruments. A good place to start would be investing in 2-4 long-term bonds, 5-10% in each.

The reason for still having the bonds is to balance the higher risk of other asset classes. However, in this case they will not be able to offset huge fluctuations as the risk exposure is not balanced enough between your assets.</td>
</tr>
<tr>
<td align="center">10%
Medium-Term
Bonds</td>
<td>For intermediate bonds the suggestion is to spread the 15% among 1-3 bonds, to your liking.</td>
</tr>
<tr>
<td align="center">10%
Short-Term
Corporate
Bonds (<3y)</td>
<td>This is a new addition to the portfolio, compared to the previous ones. With this portion of your portfolio, you provide debt capital to sustainable companies and a way to create high impact. Most of this will be via crowdfunding platforms.</td>
</tr>
<tr><td colspan="2">5% Real-Estate</td></tr>
<tr>
<td colspan="2">Real estate might seem counter intuitive. But if you can find sustainable real estate projects, for example via crowdfunding platforms, it is a good investment alternative as the need for housing will increase continuously.</td>
</tr>
</table>

25% Commodities	
15 – 20% Gold	15% of your investment should be in gold if you can afford it, preferably in Fairmined. The remainder you could put towards additional gold investments, or you can put a portion into cryptocurrency such as Bitcoin.
5 – 10% Reforestation	A minimum of 5% should be spent on reforestation projects. If you cannot find sustainable real-estate investments, you can also decide to invest all this portfolio portion into reforestation with the disadvantage of having more capital locked in long-term. You might therefore want to pick reforestation investments that are slightly shorter tenor, such as shorter investment products of Forest Finance.

Medium Risk/Impact Portfolio

Example Split

30% Equity	
Share	**Company**
0.25 – 0.5%	Tesla
0.25 – 0.5%	Vestas
0.25 – 0.5%	SunPower Corp
0.25 – 0.5%	GreenMobility
0.25 – 0.5%	REC Silicon
0.25 – 0.5%	Maxeon Solar Technologies Ltd
0.25 – 0.5%	Shimano
0.25 – 0.5%	Stericycle
0.25 – 0.5%	Umwelt Bank AG
0.25 – 0.5%	Ormat Technologies
0.25 – 0.5%	Kadant
0.25 – 0.5%	East Japan Railway
0.25 – 0.5%	Sims Metal Management
0.25 – 0.5%	Tomra Systems
0.25 – 0.5%	United Natural Foods
0.25 – 0.5%	Acciona
0.25 – 0.5%	First Solar
0.25 – 0.5%	Iberdrola
0.25 – 0.5%	NextEra
0.25 – 0.5%	Brookfield Renewable Partners

5 – 10% Stocks

	2.5 – 5%	Sustainable Accelerator	Accelerator for sustainable start-ups
0 – 5% **Early-stage** **Companies**	0.25 – 0.50%	Polysolar	Renewable Energy / Waves
	0.25 – 0.50%	Green Marine International AB	Electric transportation / Boats
	0.25 – 0.50%	Abundance	Finance / Green investment platform
	0.25 – 0.50%	Antaco	Renewable Energy / Recycling
	0.25 – 0.50%	NuW	Consumption / Clothes sharing
	0.25 – 0.50%	Unity	Electric transport / Cars
	0.25 – 0.50%	Fairphone	Consumption / Electronics
	0.25 – 0.50%	Sono motors	Electric transport / Cars
	0.25 – 0.50%	Oddbox	Food / Food Waste
	0.25 – 0.50%	Perfect World Ice Cream	Food
	0.25 – 0.50%	hiyacar	Transportation / Car sharing
	0.25 – 0.50%	We don't have time	Social Media Platform about Climate Change
	0.25 – 0.50%	Spare Fruit	Food / Food Waste
	0.25 – 0.50%	Fairafric	Food

 Medium Risk/Impact Portfolio

0.25 – 0.50%	BiOhm	Construction
0.25 – 0.50%	Lendahand	Finance / Sustainable Investments Platform
0.25 – 0.50%	Solelgrossisten (SWE)	Renewable Energy / Solar
0.25 – 0.50%	Kale United	Finance / Vegan Food
0.25 – 0.50%	Zenz	Cosmetics

5% **Index Funds**	1.25%	First Trust ISE Global Wind Energy Index Fund	Renewable Energy
	1.25%	iShares MSCI Global Impact ETF	Impact
	1.25%	Öhman Etisk Emerging Markets A	Emerging Markets
	1.25%	Öhman Global Marknad Hållbar A	Global
10% **Active Funds**	5%	CB Save Earth Fund RC	Global Impact
	5%	Triodos Global Equities Impact Fund	Global Impact

40% Bonds		
	Share	**Fund**
20% Long-term Bonds	5%	iShares € Govt Bond 15-30yr UCITS ETF EUR (Dist)
	5%	SSgA SPDR BBG Barclays 15+ Year Gilt UCITS ETF
	5%	Xtrackers II Eurozone Government Bond 15-30 UCITS ETF 1C
	5%	Xtrackers II Eurozone Government Bond 25+ UCITS ETF 1C
10% Medium-term Bonds	2.5%	Invesco Euro Government Bond 5-7 Year UCITS ETF
	5%	Ossiam Euro Government Bonds 3-5 Carbon Reduction - UCITS ETF 1C
	2.5%	iShares Global Inflation Linked Govt Bond UCITS ETF USD
10% Short-term Corporate Bonds	2%	Trine
	2%	GLS Crowd
	2%	Abundance
	2%	SunExchange
	2%	Energize Africa

5% Real-Estate		
Investment Platforms	2.5%	Reinvest24
	2.5%	CrowdEstate

25% Commodities		
20% Gold	**10%**	**Gold on BullionVault**
	5%	WisdomTree Physical Swiss Gold ETC
	5%	Fairmined Gold via Fairever
5% Reforestation	2.5%	Forest Finance
	2.5%	World Tree

Medium Risk/Impact Portfolio

High Risk/Impact Portfolio

Liquidity	★★★½☆
Additionality	★★★★☆
Environment	★★★★☆
Social	★★★★☆
Transparency	★★★★☆
Effort	★★★½☆
Risk	★★½☆☆
Return	★★★½☆

Mind Your Money

This portfolio option is less of a risk diversification but rather a focus on positive and additive impact.

This portfolio suits a person that can take a high-risk investment strategy with an increased possibility of loss to make a majority of the portfolio very active and high impact regarding climate change.

This is the riskiest and most illiquid portfolio of the examples mentioned and should only be considered if the loss of the invested capital is something that you are willing to risk.

The split can look as follows:

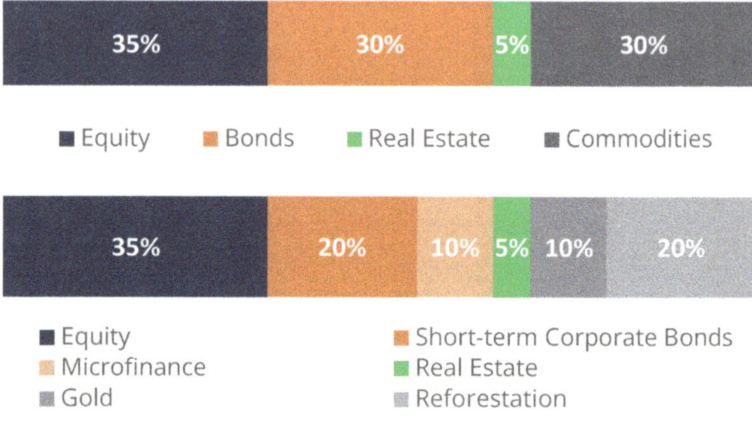

The bonds are split in:
- 20% short-term corporate bonds (<3 years)
- 10% microfinance

and the commodities consist of:
- 5-10% gold
- 20 – 25% reforestation
- Small portions of cryptocurrency if interested.

In each of the sub-categories you want to ensure additional adequate diversification. As for example investing all your equity capital only in one company would make this even more volatile. The level of sub-diversification also depends on how much work you want to spend on managing your investments, in particular the re-balancing element of it.

Whatever portion of your capital you have not allocated to an investment class, you want to put in a liquid savings account, preferably with an ethical bank as discussed earlier. This enables you to draw down money when needed without affecting your portfolio.

35% Equity	
5% Stocks	You can invest 5% of your total capital into stocks such as Tesla or a solar company. The reason this is reduced to 5% is that it is not an active part of your investments and that it requires more time to manage. With a high impact portfolio, you want to make as much additional impact as possible, therefore focusing more on the early-stage portion.
10 – 15% Early-stage Companies	As early-stage companies are often creating real change, this is one of the most active parts of your investment portfolio and in this example takes a bigger share. This is a higher risk asset. Therefore, you should be aware that the higher your exposure is here the more unbalanced will be your final portfolio.
5% Index Funds	We have minimized our exposure to index funds as they are the least active part of the equity portfolio. You could even eliminate them if you wish.
10 – 15% Active Funds	Active funds are more expensive, but also better in allocating capital to companies that try to make a true difference - and therefore more sustainable. You can vary this percentage up to 15% if you deem the extra costs worth the environmental benefit.

<table>
<tr><td colspan="2">

30% Bonds

The reason that bonds have been reduced in this portfolio is that we need to make place for more active and transparent investment assets and bonds rank terrible in both criteria. The reason for still having the bonds is to balance the higher risk of other asset classes. However, in this case they will not be able to offset huge fluctuations as the risk exposure is not balanced enough between your assets.

</td></tr>
<tr><td>

15% Short-Term Corporate Bonds (<3y)

</td><td>

As previously, you want to provide debt capital to sustainable companies, best via crowdfunding platforms. This is the most active part of your bond asset class.

</td></tr>
<tr><td>

15% Micro-finance

</td><td>

This is the first portfolio introducing microfinance. As it is a very specific investment opportunity and high impact, it replaces the other bond alternatives.

</td></tr>
<tr><td colspan="2">

5% Real-Estate

</td></tr>
<tr><td colspan="2">

Real estate might seem counter intuitive. But if you can find sustainable real estate projects via, for example, crowdfunding platforms it is a good investment alternative as the need for housing will increase continuously.

</td></tr>
<tr><td colspan="2">

30% Commodities

</td></tr>
<tr><td>

10% Gold

</td><td>

5% of your investment should be in gold if you can afford it, preferably in Fairmined. The remainder you could put towards additional gold investments, or you can put a portion into cryptocurrency such as Bitcoin.

</td></tr>
<tr><td>

20% Reforestation

</td><td>

The reforestation portion is increased here again as they are likely the highest impact part of your entire investment portfolio.

</td></tr>
</table>

Example Split

35% Equity		
	Share	**Company**
5% Stocks	0.25%	Tesla
	0.25%	Vestas
	0.25%	SunPower Corp
	0.25%	GreenMobility
	0.25%	REC Silicon
	0.25%	Maxeon Solar Technologies Ltd
	0.25%	Shimano
	0.25%	Stericycle
	0.25%	Umwelt Bank AG
	0.25%	Ormat Technologies
	0.25%	Kadant
	0.25%	East Japan Railway
	0.25%	Sims Metal Management
	0.25%	Tomra Systems
	0.25%	United Natural Foods
	0.25%	Acciona
	0.25%	First Solar
	0.25%	Iberdrola
	0.25%	NextEra
	0.25%	Brookfield Renewable Partners

	5%	Sustainable Accelerator	Accelerator for sustainable start-ups
	0.50%	Polysolar	Renewable Energy / Waves
	0.50%	Green Marine International AB	Electric transportation
	0.50%	Abundance	Green Investments
	0.50%	Antaco	Renewable Energy / Recycling
	0.50%	NuW	Consumption / Clothes sharing
	0.50%	Unity	Electric transport
15%	0.50%	Fairphone	Electronics
	0.50%	Sono motors	Electric transport
Early-stage	0.50%	Oddbox	Food / Food Waste
	0.50%	Perfect World Ice Cream	Food
Companies	0.50%	hiyacar	Transportation
	0.50%	We don't have time	Social Media Platform about Climate Change
	0.50%	Spare Fruit	Food / Food Waste
	0.50%	Fairafric	Food
	0.50%	BiOhm	Construction
	0.50%	Lendahand	Sustainable Investments
	0.50%	Solelgrossisten (SWE)	Renewable Energy
	0.50%	Kale United	Vegan Food
	0.50%	Zenz	Cosmetics
	0.5%	Sharetribe	Platform for sharing marketplaces

5% Index Funds	1.25%	First Trust ISE Global Wind Energy Index Fund	Renewable Energy
	1.25%	iShares MSCI Global Impact ETF	Impact
	1.25%	Öhman Etisk Emerging Markets A	Emerging Markets
	1.25%	Öhman Global Marknad Hållbar A	Global
10% Active Funds	5%	CB Save Earth Fund RC	Global Impact
	5%	Triodos Global Equities Impact Fund	Global Impact
40% Bonds			
10% Micro-finance	5%	Oikocredit	
	5%	Lendahand	
20% Short-term Corporate Bonds	3%	Trine	
	3%	GLS Crowd	
	3%	Abundance	
	3%	SunExchange	
	3%	Energize Africa	
	5%	EU – Triodos Euro Bond Impact Fund	
5% Real-Estate			
Investment Platforms	2.5%	Reinvest24	
	2.5%	CrowdEstate	
25% Commodities			
10% Gold/Bitcoin	**4%**	**Gold on BullionVault**	
	3%	Fairmined Gold via Fairever	
	3%	Bitcoin	
20% Reforestation	10%	Forest Finance	
	10%	World Tree	

 High Risk/Impact Portfolio

VI – Conclusion

Mind Your Money

Taking a sustainable approach to investing is neither simple nor straightforward (yet). The idea of this book is to show you alternatives for investment to improve the impact of your money on people and planet and hopefully begin to broker discussions around how this type of investing could, and should, be the norm for everyone's portfolios. My goal has been to provide you with some ideas and inspiration to "greenen" your own investment portfolio and divest part or all your money into more sustainable investments.

And yes, what I've presented is neither a silver bullet nor is it perfect. The options described are not radical and the portfolios mentioned in the end still will contain portions of capital that might not be in its "perfect" environmental place. Its idea is to be attractive to most everyday investors. It is an improvement over the status quo and if you feel strongly about taking further action, you are more than welcome to do so.

It is important to have a clear intention with your investment strategy and ask yourself why you are investing as it will guide your investment decisions. Analyze your existing investments and identify which of them you need to divest yourself from. After having made a breakdown of what you want to invest in, you should move your capital over a 3 to 6 months period to ensure an acceptable risk exposure to different market pricing through dollar-cost-averaging. And as much as possible, try to automate your investments.

To ensure a minimum risk exposure it will be crucial to diversify your investments in as many different asset types as possible with the time you have to spend managing your investments. As you will have to re-balance your portfolio several times a year, a more diverse portfolio will add more time to manage the assets. To be able to re-balance your portfolio you should also ensure to have a way to track your investments.

To invest truly sustainable, you need to look at the environmental, social, and economic impact of your investments. None of those three can be ignored in your investment decisions. Based on these three segments, each asset you invest in should be assessed and fit your investment strategy. Some assets will be easier to understand than others and you should assume that if you cannot fully understand the asset you are investing in it is not as sustainable as you might think.

The blend of assets to pick for your portfolio depends on your investment focus. Generally, a mix of equity, bonds, commodities, and some alternative investments provides a good risk diversification, depending on the individual asset's risk profiles. Each asset shall be rated by answering the questions that we mentioned int the ratings chapter in the beginning and with the rating tool provided in the end of the book you can get a picture of the portfolio rating based on how much of your capital you want to invest in each asset.

At the end it is up to each of us to decide how much risk we are willing to take to invest in a sustainable future. Not everybody is going to be comfortable with putting in big portions of their capital into start-ups, cryptocurrency or even reforestation. However, it is also clear that the riskiest future will be the one where no-one is willing to finance these sustainable options and we all stick to a status quo that is not sustainable, economically, environmentally, or socially. In such a future any investment, including the ones in fossil fuels will not only underperform but be non-performing and default. That's why we need a divestment movement for the average investor, not just pension and endowment funds. Putting your money where your mouth is has never been more important than now.

Thanks to services such as crowd-investing sites and an increasingly accessible investment landscape, we have more options to invest in than ever before. Yes, most of these services might not be fully automatable yet, but there are services coming available that do just that. Digital technology has enabled us to start democratizing a space that has been partly fenced off before.

I also want to note that sustainable investing is not an invitation to free-ride the system and avoid changing other parts of your life. It has one of the biggest potentials to make a difference and should therefore be the prioritized action we all can take tomorrow. But once implemented, we must also look at ourselves and consider other lifestyle changes we can make over the coming years. These can range from changing one's consumption patterns (buying new versus second-hand), ways of traveling (local transportation versus by airplane) to diet choices (meat versus mostly vegetarian). We need to change our societies and behaviors from the ground up and that involves most aspects of our daily lives.

Being part of the system, we will encourage politicians to be braver if we as individuals start a change. We can start a chain reaction by providing the needed support to a new wave of companies that include people and the planet in their business model. Each one of us can be a change-maker if we are just willing to do the work and educate ourselves about our choices.

But I know you are not naive. The burden of transformation necessary is on an unprecedented scale that cannot rest on the work of individuals only. What matters in the end is that big societal shifts are happening and are happening on time. We need to vote for politicians that have a clear vision of a green future. We must demand from them to do the hard work of changing entire systems. We need to advocate that corporations need to change how they do business and remove wrong incentives that encourage negative behavior. This includes replacement of taxes and subsidies that still favor non-sustainable options.

We need to stop big portions of our fossil fuel subsidies and introduce carbon taxes to put the external costs caused by these goods and services into the price. We need to support small-scale agriculture and start phasing out the idea that big agriculture is the most efficient way of producing food in the future. We need to stop supporting transport options such as air travel with tax breaks and cheap fuel and move this monetary support to options such as high-speed trains.

In the end we will need to rethink our approach and the capital system we are living in. Can we sustain infinite growth on a finite planet forever? Probably not - the math would say so at least. Yes, there might be options such as asteroid mining and colonizing planets. But let's be realistic, these options will not be viable before we have fixed the climate crisis. Reinventing the wheel completely might not be necessary though.

Rather, we need to consider how our capitalistic system can be upgraded - not replaced. How we can be more efficient with our resources from an environmental perspective. Shipping food products between four different countries to get a product to a customer is not only inefficient environmentally, without the fossil fuel horsepower behind, it will also be economically challenging.

Yes, it can seem overwhelming to change so many aspects of our lives and seemingly must overturn how we have lived in the last few hundred years. Personally, you do not have to do everything at once. Yes, speed is important. More important than speed is however consistency and actual implementation.

If you want to pick only one action to get started and keep it simple, let it be your money and your investments. Through them you have the biggest impact imaginable on our common future. Your money will not only work for yourself, but for all of society and the planet. Acting will help remove some of the anxieties that we are building up in these times of necessary radical change and increasing mismatch of where we need to be and where we currently are. Once you have set foot in the right direction, further action will feel less daunting. And then we will see a more positive picture of the future ahead of us and our children.

We will see that the future can be exciting and something to look forward to. After all, we still have the chance to undo the damage we have inflicted on the planet and the environment and live on a planet with wild nature around us. We can ensure to live in a future with clean air, clean water, healthy food, equality, and opportunities for all of humanity. We can have a future with less of a divide between people inside our countries and between the northern and southern hemispheres. And we can have an economy that supports all that, with businesses that do not only look at the monetary, quarterly bottom-line, but that take their responsibility towards societies and the environment serious and as a part of their business model.

All we need to do is use the power of our choices wisely and choose consistently investments, products and services that support the future we want to see. By being the change we want to see and changing our habits we are then able to co-create this positive future together. Money is in the end just a different form of energy and we must start directing our societies' energies towards a brighter future that we can look forward to.

About the Author

Andreas Lehner is a global citizen with a passion for sustainability.

He's a serial climate entrepreneur, having co-founded ventures tackling sustainability issues such as renewable energy finance in emerging markets (Trine) and methane removal (Powerblocks). With over a decade of experience in entrepreneurship and sustainability, Andreas mentors startups and entrepreneurs on their own journeys.

He is committed to inspiring positive change and youth leadership in sustainable development, as an advocate for a more sustainable world and in his role as entrepreneur, coach, and author.

Appendices

Reviews

Thank you for reading "Mind your money". If you enjoyed this book, please visit the site where you purchased it and write a brief review. Your feedback is important to me and will help other readers decide whether to read the book too. Also, please spread the word if you think more people should learn about how to make their capital have more impact.

If you'd like to get deeper into sustainable investments, I suggest you have a look at my organization offers at https://andreas-lehner.com. Through it I spread knowledge about sustainable investing to a wider audience through coaching, investment newsletters and other ways still in development.

Feel free to reach out to me via hi@andreas-lehner.com and on https://andreas-lehner.com

Wishing you the best!

Andreas

Additional Material

As much of what was discussed in this book requires tools to implement and manage, I want to provide you with a set of tools that can make it easier to get started and to manage your investments initially.

Investment Portfolio Management

To manage your investments continuously, you will need to have a clear overview of how much you have invested and where. This can be a daunting task, in particular if you are considering using many different investment platforms.

To ease the pain, I have created a sheet that you can use to track your investments. Send me an email to hi@andreas-lehner.com and you get a copy.

It allows you to:
- Manage many different platforms in one place
- See the value of your portfolio in real-time
- Re-balance your portfolio on a continuous basis
- Ease investing with the dollar-cost-averaging method

Investment Rating System

As we have seen in the previous chapters, being able to rate your investments can give you a clearer idea of what you are intending to invest in. It is not a scientific tool of course, but rather a tool to see in which area the investment opportunity performs best.

- Simple overview of all assets mentioned in the book
- Rating sheet template
- Examples of best cases in each rating category

Investment Coaching

And if looking at tangible investment options yourself is still not simplified enough, I also offer investment coaching to individuals that want to understand the sustainability of their investment portfolios and get tangible suggestion on what to change to make them more sustainable.

More on that at hi@andreas-lehner.com

Decimal Ratings

Asset Ratings

		Liquidity	Additionality	Environment	Social	Transparency	Time	Risk	Return
Equity	Public Stocks	5	3	4	4	4	3.5	3	4
	Index Funds	5	1.5	1	1	1	4	4	4
	Active Funds	5	3.5	4	4	2.5	4	4	3.5
	Private Stocks	3	5	5	5	4.5	2.5	1	5
Commodities	Gold	5	1	1.5	1.5	5	4	4	3.5
	Crypto	5	2	1.5	3.5	5	2	1	5
	Forest	1	5	5	5	5	4	3	3
Real Estate		3	2.5	3.5	3.5	5	3	3	4
Bonds	Government	4	2	2	2.5	1	3	5	3
	Corporate	4.5	3.5	4	4	3	3.5	3	3
	Corporate Crowdfunding	2	5	5	5	4.5	2	2	3
	Microfinance	5	4.5	3	4	3.5	3	1	3

Portfolio Ratings

	Low Risk	Medium Risk	High Risk
Liquidity	4.5	4.2	3.4
Additionality	2.1	2.6	4
Environment	2.3	2.9	3.9
Social	2.5	3.1	4.1
Transparency	2	3	4.1
Time	3.5	3.6	3.3
Risk	4.5	4	2.6
Return	3.3	3.4	3.6

 Decimal Ratings

Endnotes

---

[1]   https://www.nordea.com/en/sustainability/sustainability-news/nordeas-illustrative-analysis-on-carbon-footprint-from-savings.html   and https://www.nordea.com/Images/33-282871/Sustainable%20Finance%20at%20Nordea.pdf

[2]   https://funds.rbcgam.com/_assets-custom/pdf/RBC-GAM-does-SRI-hurt-investment-returns.pdf

[3]   https://www.ft.com/content/95efca74-4299-11ea-a43a-c4b328d9061c   and https://theenergymix.com/2020/03/04/1-5c-warming-means-breathtaking-900-billion-loss-for-colossal-fossils

[4] https://www.mckinsey.com/business-functions/sustainability/our-insights/will-mortgages-and-markets-stay-afloat-in-florida#

[5] IPCC, 2013:Climate Change 2013: The Physical Science Basis. Contribution of Working Group I to the Fifth Assessment Report of the Intergovernmental Panel on Climate Change[Stocker, T.F., D. Qin, G.-K. Plattner, M. Tignor, S.K. Allen, J. Boschung, A. Nauels, Y. Xia, V. Bex and P.M. Midgley (eds.)]. Cambridge University Press, Cambridge, United Kingdom and New York, NY, USA, 1535 pp.

[6] Bernhard Bereiter, Sarah Eggleston, Jochen Schmitt, Christoph Nehrbass-Ahles, Thomas F. Stocker, Hubertus Fischer, Sepp Kipfstuhl and Jerome Chappellaz. 2015. Revision of the EPICA Dome C CO2 record from 800 to 600 kyr before present.*Geophysical Research Letters*. . doi: 10.1002/2014GL061957

[7] UNEP (United Nations Environment Programme). 2019. *Emissions Gap Report 2019*.   Nairobi: UNEP. https://wedocs.unep.org/bitstream/handle/20.500.11822/30797/EGR2019.pdf?sequence=1&isAllowed=y

[8] IPCC (Intergovernmental Panel on Climate Change). 2018. Summary for Policymakers. In *Global Warming of 1.5°C: An IPCC Special Report*. Geneva: World Meteorological   Organization. https://www.ipcc.ch/site/assets/uploads/sites/2/2018/07/SR15_SPM_version_stand_alone_LR.pdf; https://www.ipcc.ch/sr15/

[9] https://www.epa.gov/smm/advancing-sustainable-materials-management-facts-and-figures

[10] https://www.nationalgeographic.com/environment/habitats/plastic-pollution

[11] https://www.stateofglobalair.org/health/newborns

[12]

https://www.banktrack.org/download/why_to_integrate_sustainability_criteria_in_financial_regulation

[13]   https://www.morganstanley.com/articles/dollar-cost-averaging-lump-sum-investing

[14]   https://www.atmosfair.de/en/the-additionality-problem-of-carbon-offset-projects

[15] Washington Trust Bank Wealth Management & Advisory Services. "Do Commodities Add Value to Portfolio Performance," Page 4. Accessed May 22, 2020.

[16] https://www.fairmined.org/

[17] https://www.sciencedirect.com/science/article/pii/S0301420717301484

[18] https://www.economist.com/the-economist-explains/2018/07/09/why-bitcoin-uses-so-much-energy

[19] https://ccaf.io/cbnsi/cbeci/ghg

[20] https://cointelegraph.com/news/bitcoin-clean-energy-usage-exceeds-50-percent-tesla-accepting-btc-payments

[21] https://www.youtube.com/watch?v=2T0OUIW89Il

[22] https://www.reuters.com/article/us-venezuela-economy/venezuela-annual-inflation-hits-24600-percent-in-may-national-assembly-idUSKBN1J71YB

[23] https://www.lawfareblog.com/cryptocurrency-and-dismantling-terrorism-financing-campaigns

[24] https://en.wikipedia.org/wiki/Mt._Gox

[25] https://science.sciencemag.org/content/365/6448/76

[26] https://www.theguardian.com/environment/2019/jul/04/planting-billions-trees-best-tackle-climate-crisis-scientists-canopy-emissions

[27] GLOBAL STATUS REPORT 2017 - World Green Building Council https://www.worldgbc.org/sites/default/files/UNEP%20188_GABC_en%20%28web%29.pdf

[28] https://www.risklab.com/media/151208_esg_in_real_estate.pdf

[29] Impact in Motion (2014)

[30] https://www.robecosam.com/en/key-strengths/country-sustainability-ranking.html

[31] https://edition.cnn.com/2018/10/11/asia/bhutan-carbon-negative/index.html

[32] https://www.government.se/press-releases/2019/07/state-to-issue-green-bonds-by-2020/

[33] https://money.cnn.com/retirement/guide/investing_bonds.moneymag/index3.htm

[34] Asian Development Bank. Microenterprise Development: Not by Credit Alone. Asian Development Bank (ADB), Manila, 1997. https://citeseerx.ist.psu.edu/document?repid=rep1&type=pdf&doi=569182078e61f1c1c3310afc1a084f98ee169780

[35] http://elibrary.worldbank.org/doi/pdf/10.1596/1813-9450-6821

[36] https://www.investopedia.com/articles/financial-advisors/011916/why-6040-portfolio-no-longer-good-enough.asp

9 789819 891889